Legends *of* Animation

Walter
Lantz

Legends of Animation

Tex Avery:
Hollywood's Master of Screwball Cartoons

Walt Disney:
The Mouse that Roared

Matt Groening:
From Spitballs to Springfield

William Hanna and Joseph Barbera:
The Sultans of Saturday Morning

Walter Lantz:
Made Famous by a Woodpecker

John Lasseter:
The Whiz Who Made Pixar King

Hayao Miyazaki:
Japan's Premier Anime Storyteller

Genndy Tartakovsky:
From Russia to Coming-of-Age Animator

Legends *of* Animation

Walter Lantz

Made Famous by a Woodpecker

Jeff Lenburg

CHELSEA HOUSE
An Infobase Learning Company

Walter Lantz: Made Famous by a Woodpecker

Chelsea House
An Infobase Learning Company
132 West 31st Street
New York NY 10001

Library of Congress Cataloging-in-Publication Data
Lenburg, Jeff.
  Walter Lantz : made famous by a woodpecker / Jeff Lenburg. — 1st ed.
     p. cm. — (Legends of animation)
  Includes bibliographical references and index.
  ISBN-13: 978-1-60413-839-9 (hardcover : alk. paper)
  ISBN-10: 1-60413-839-4 (hardcover : alk. paper) 1. Lantz, Walter—Biography—Juvenile literature. 2. Animators—United States—Biography—Juvenile literature. I. Lantz, Walter. II. Title. III. Series.
  NC1766.U52L365 2011
  791.43092—dc23
  [B]   2011026687

Chelsea House books are available at special discounts when purchased in bulk quantities for businesses, associations, institutions, or sales promotions. Please call our Special Sales Department in New York at (212) 967-8800 or (800) 322-8755.

You can find Chelsea House on the World Wide Web at
http://www.infobaselearning.com

Text design by Kerry Casey
Cover design by Takeshi Takahashi
Composition by EJB Publishing Services
Cover printed by IBT Global, Troy, N.Y.
Book printed and bound by IBT Global, Troy, N.Y.
Date printed: December 2011

Printed in the United States of America

10 9 8 7 6 5 4 3 2 1

This book is printed on acid-free paper.

All links and Web addresses were checked and verified to be correct at the time of publication. Because of the dynamic nature of the Web, some addresses and links may have changed since publication and may no longer be valid.

To my dear friends, Dick and Kathy,
and their bird to beat all birds (even Woody), Jake

CONTENTS

ACKNOWLEDGMENTS

First and foremost, I would like to personally thank the late Walter Lantz for his kindness, generosity, encouragement, and support, and for sharing his memories, insights, and material that became the basis of my formative chapter on his career for my book *The Great Cartoon Directors*, and were largely helpful in producing this more expanded look into his life and achievements in the art of animation.

My sincere thanks to the staffs of the Margaret Herrick Library of the Academy of Motion Picture Arts and Sciences; the Archives of Performing Arts and the Regional History Collections at the University of Southern California; Arizona State University Fletcher Library at the West Campus; the Los Angeles Times Photographic Archive of the University of California, Los Angeles Library; Associated Press; and United Press International, for the use of research, oral histories, interview transcripts, books and articles, photographs, and other documents vital to the success of this project.

My deepest gratitude to numerous publications as well, including the *Los Angeles Times*, the *New York Times*, *Daily Mirror*, *American Film*, *Box Office*, *Classic Images*, *Film Daily*, *Films in Review*, *Hollywood Reporter*, *Motion Picture Herald*, *Showman's Trade Review*, and *Variety*, for their coverage of the subject's life and achievements that was a tremendous asset in the researching and writing of this biography.

1

Drawing
for Laughs

I n New York City, the birthplace of American animation, he helped
pioneer a fledgling art form from the ground floor up into a boom-
ing industry. Before cartoons "talked," he brought favorites from the
Sunday comic pages to life on the silver screen and produced some of
animation's most memorable silent films. He even created, produced,
and directed his own famous characters, establishing him as one of the
great animators of his time. Then entering into a partnership that lasted
nearly 60 years, one of the longest producer-studio relationships in the
annals of show business, he produced and directed one of the earliest
and most successful sound cartoon series, *Oswald the Lucky Rabbit*, and
created his own stable of stars: the lovable Andy Panda, Chilly Willy,
Gabby Gator, and others. His most famous creation would endear him
to generations of audiences in every language and around the world: the
machine-gun laughing, off-the-charts, feathered friend Woody Woodpecker. That man made famous by a woodpecker was Walter Lantz.

Born on April 27, 1899, in New Rochelle, New York, Walter was
the first child of Francesco "Frank" Paolo Lanza (given the surname
of Lantz after immigrating to the United States) and the former Mary

Gervasi (changed to the homogenized Jarvis to avoid prejudice). Walter's father was a tough-minded and practical man who ran his own butcher shop, and his mother was warm and loving and an accomplished pianist. Walter and his parents all lived under the same roof in his grandfather Michael Jarvis' elegant two-story home—a loud, boisterous, and loving Italian household. There Walter was surrounded by old world values, as well as music and song as his three uncles, his aunt, and his mother held jam sessions every Sunday, with neighbors joining in on the food, music, and free wine. "Sometimes we'd have fifty mothers and fathers and kids, and we'd have a heck of a time," Walter later wrote.

Walter's mother delivered a second son, Alfredo, and later gave birth to Walter's youngest brother, Michael, but she died two weeks after the birth, before Walter reached his teens. Her sudden passing sent shockwaves through the family. Grief-stricken, Frank took his two sons Walter and Alfredo to live with his brother Tony, and left baby Michael in the care of his sister-in-law Carrie. As if Walter's mother's death wasn't enough, after a severe bout of rheumatism caused severe pain and swelling in his knees, Frank was left incapacitated and unable to stand, walk, or move his legs. In 1911, at age 12, Walter learned the principles of business firsthand by working in a commissary with his disabled father as his boss, feeding 50 fellow countrymen who were working at a new stone quarry in Beckley, Connecticut.

Walter never let his boyhood responsibilities get in the way of pursuing his dreams. After hours at night he filled his time doing one of his favorite pastimes: drawing and copying early popular comic strips like *The Yellow Kid*, *The Katzenjammer Kids*, and *Bringing Up Father*. As he once recalled, "Some men never do learn what they want to do. I knew at 12. I wanted to be an artist."

In 1913, Walter took Zimmerman mail-order cartooning courses at the encouragement of his father who paid the hefty $30 course fee, not wanting to see his talented son toil away in a commissary in a stone mine his entire life. Those lessons later proved vital to Walter's success as an animator. After successfully completing Zimmernan's course, he took many others that were offered. As Walter added, "I took all there were."

A year after the stone quarry closed, Frank, Walter, and Alfredo moved back to New Rochelle and boarded with their uncle Tony. In 1914, at 15, Walter landed a job as "grease monkey" at a local garage, and there his months of correspondence art school training eventually paid off. He found much "humor" from working with other mechanics, which inspired him to create many comical doodles that he posted on the shop's bulletin board. His hilarious drawings caught the attention of many customers, including Fred Kafka, a former Yale graduate and ex-athlete-turned-successful contractor who brought his mustard-yellow Stutz Bearcat in to be serviced. Kafka was impressed not only by the diminutive artist's conscientiousness but also by his funny drawings. The goggled and scarf-laden Kafka, who would be responsible for setting young Walter on the path to fulfill his dreams, told him, "Walter, you're wasting your time in this garage. I'd like to pay your tuition to go to Art Students League in New York and get a really good art background."

Thanks to Kafka, every night at five o'clock after finishing work, Walter would quickly clean up, wolf down dinner, and take the commuter train into the city—a 45-minute trip one way—to attend George Bridgeman's anatomy class at the Art Students League on 57th Street six nights a week. His first night of class became a rude awakening as the eager and somewhat sheltered teen and his fellow students were taught how to draw "live nudes" of a "plump model" who sat naked on a stool the entire time as they rendered charcoal drawings of her. As Walter confessed to biographer Joe Adamson, "My charcoal pencil could hardly touch the paper."

BEGINNING HIS CARTOON DREAMS

After months of balancing such a demanding schedule, Walter almost gave up. Kafka once again intervened. That year, in 1914, he wrote a letter of introduction to an old Yale buddy at the New York *American* newspaper, then the daily morning edition of the New York *Journal* and both owned by legendary newspaper mogul William Randolph Hearst. Kafka's friend hired Walter as an office boy at a starting salary of $7 a week. Even as young as he was, he had a respect for money and knew how to handle it. "I never had any difficulty getting along on $7 a week," he later said.

Leaving his family behind in New Rochelle, Walter moved to New York City, securing a bedbug-infested room at the YMCA at 125th Street for $2 a week. He made a decent enough wage to buy a delicious seven-course dinner at any number of Jewish, Italian, or Polish restaurants in Harlem for a mere 35 cents and still had ample "pocket change" left-over at the end of the week.

While the work he did wasn't "glamorous," Walter made the most of the opportunity and soon became a jack-of-all-trades. The well-groomed and energetic young teen made a good impression handling every task without fail, whether it was running copy and proofs to editors or cleaning the brushes of artists on staff. (Among his many other duties, Walter claimed he delivered "love letters" from Hearst to actress Marion Davies, the silent screen legend with whom Hearst carried on a romantic relationship for many years but never married.) Consequently he rubbed elbows with many notable artists and comic-strip artisans who worked for the paper: George Kerr and Willy Pogany, who became famous for the exquisite covers on the Sunday *American Weekly*; George McManus, the creator of *Bringing Up Father*; James Swinnerton, who fathered the strip *Little Jimmy*; Frederick Burr Opper, inventor of *Happy Hooligan* and *Maude the Mule*; Walter Hoban of *Jerry on the Job* fame; Thomas ("Tad") A. Dorgan, best known for his stick-figure strip *Daffydils*; and George Herriman, the man behind *Krazy Kat*. Many delighted in critiquing Walter's inventive drawings, which he drew at night and brought with him to work. Eventually some of the artists entrusted the aspiring artist to do small lettering and touch-up jobs to gain invaluable firsthand experience. "They let me do an occasional lettering job," Walter once said, "and gradually let me draw some characters in their comic strips."

Walter was quickly rewarded for his hard work and value to the company. Only two months after his hiring, he was given a substantial

Walter Lantz poses with his manic woodpecker, Woody, in one of his favorite promotional stills of the two. *(Courtesy: Walter Lantz) © Walter Lantz Productions. All rights reserved.*

boost in pay to $10 a week. He believed he was on his way to becoming an artist like his famous mentors, but somehow things did not quite work out that way. He was in the right place to launch his career but with all the artist positions at the *American* taken, he went in a different direction to fulfill his dreams.

Around that time New York City was establishing itself as a major production hub of original film animation well before animation came into prominence on the West Coast. Many key figures responsible for pioneering the industry were based in the Manhattan area: people like John Randolph (J.R.) Bray, Earl Hurd, and Raoul Barré who founded the first real cartoon studios. Things began to manifest for the young cartoon industry following a major turn of events in mid-December 1915 after William Randolph Hearst, who owned the *American* and many other newspapers, jumped into the fray, opening his own cartoon studio in New York. International Film Service (IFS), an offshoot of Hearst's famed International News Service (later renamed King Features) was to produce animated short subjects based on comic strips he syndicated for theatrical distribution. The studio, located at 729 Seventh Avenue, was housed in the same building as dozens of other film offices.

When opportunity came knocking, Walter pounced on it. Knowing of his pent-up desire to become a cartoonist, the *American's* editor, Morrill Goddard—best known for inventing that great American institution, the Sunday color comics section, for the New York *World* in 1895—put the wheels into motion. After suggesting Walter apply for a job at Hearst's new studio, he recommended Walter to the man Hearst put in charge of the operation: Gregory La Cava. The 24-year-old artist had toiled at various odd jobs at the Barré studio in 1913, after working as a caricaturist and illustrator, and would later establish himself as a top-rate feature film director of classic movies such as *My Man Godfrey* (1936). La Cava hired Walter as a camera operator, and the job became his gateway into the world of animation. As Walter later recalled, "I started out in camera when I was 16. Within three years, I was an animator."

Later discussing the sequence of events that led to landing the entry-level job, Walter said in an interview that Goddard "called me to his office and told me about the studio that was to be set up by Hearst. He said I'd be paid $10 a week [the same salary he was making in his current position. As Lantz later told author Joe Adamson, "It seems I was stuck with this ten dollars a week."] He also told me a close friend of his, Gregory La Cava, would be in charge of the studio." As Goddard told the fledgling cartoonist, "You'll get in on the ground floor of a new business."

Given his release from the *American*, Walter began working in the animation department under La Cava and a small but growing staff of artists. He quickly ascended from camera operator to inker and then to assistant animator by the time he turned 18. Assisting La Cava and his team of animators, he helped animate many popular characters from the comic pages of Hearst's newspapers, bringing them to movie screens, including *Bringing Up Father, Happy Hooligan, Krazy Kat*, and *The Katzenjammer Kids*, fulfilling his unflinching desire to become a full-fledged animator by age 19. He was not the only staff member new to the industry who did not know how to animate. Several of his associates—including Vernon Stallings (later going under the name of George Stallings), Bill Nolan, Jack King, Frank Moser, and John Foster—all learned how to animate cartoons with him. As Walter once stated, "We didn't know much about animation in those days— everything was loose and rubbery—but my studies at the Art Students League had given me a good background in drawing the figure in various positions."

He and his colleagues "learned by doing," as he once said. They took live-action footage of regular people, and projecting the images frame by frame, they drew outlines of the images and learned how to make a character take a step in eight frames. Walter also projected silent film comedies of Charlie Chaplin, tracing them frame by frame, and then flipping the drawings to study his motions. In an interview, Walter remarked, "All they knew how to do was walk a character from left to right. If they were going to make them talk, they'd animate their mouth with four drawings and hold a balloon over their head to give the audience enough time to read what the character was saying. That was the extent of their training."

TAKING THE HELM

In 1918, the outbreak of World War I wreaked havoc on Hearst's thriving cartoon enterprise as well as the rest of the industry as many animators were drafted into the armed services. At Hearst's International Film Service, the staff was so badly depleted by the draft that only two were left—young Walter, who was spared because he was underage, and La Cava. As a result, La Cava turned over the entire production of the *Jerry on the Job* cartoon series to Walter to direct. The series was adapted from the black-inked, five-panel strip created in 1912, for the *New York Journal* by a relatively unknown 25-year-old reporter-turned-professional comic artist, Walter C. Hoban. The strip followed the adventures of a diminutive yet resourceful 10-year-old office boy. Stallings originally animated and co-directed the series with La Cava beginning in June 1916. Prior to Lantz's reign as director, the cartoons appeared as part of the weekly *Hearst-Vitagraph News Pictorials*, a series of live-action theatrical newsreels on popular events mixed with cartoon shorts. "I animated one 250-foot *Jerry on the Job* every two weeks," Lantz recalls. "The drawings in those days were black and white on paper. We'd pencil the drawings, then ink them in, and photograph each sheet."

That year, Walter did so well with the series that La Cava assigned him to animate *Tad Cartoons*, a series of short silhouettes that played at the end of the Hearst newsreels. They were based on Hearst newspaper cartoonist Thomas Dorgan's humorous feature *Daffydils*, beginning with the first release, *Tad's Little Daffydills*. By then La Cava brought on board another staffer, William "Bill" Nolan, with whom Lantz would forge a long-lasting partnership when he later opened his own studio. Nolan had previously worked for Edison Studios filming live-action advertisements before teaming with cartoonist Raoul Barré in 1913 to try producing a cartoon together. Later that year Walter codirected with Nolan a second release, *Tad's Indoor Sports*, a comic-to-screen version of Dorgan's popular sports panel of the same name.

Unlike his previous efforts for Hearst's International Film Service, Walter's *Tad Cartoons* did not produce a thunderous response or anything of lasting value like the studio's ongoing series starring established comic strip stars of the day. It would become IFS's last cartoon series as Hearst, due to financial problems, was forced to shut down the studio in July of that year. Discovering that producing film cartoon shorts was not nearly as profitable as he first believed, Hearst pulled out before producing further efforts put him deeper into debt.

As a result, Walter lost his job, as did many other staffers. Once again, however, good fortune smiled down on him with the right door opening at the right time, leading him to greater success.

Winning Over His Rivals

Losing his job with Hearst was certainly a crushing blow, especially considering how much he toiled with limited resources and staff to make his cartoons successful, but Walter recovered and was soon back among the employed.

For a short time Walter worked as an animator at the Barré-Bowers Studio, founded by cartoonists Raoul Barré and Charles Bowers. There he animated one-reeled adventures of cartoonist Bud Fisher's *Mutt and Jeff* comic strip. He stayed until his reputation enabled him to land a job elsewhere. Many of his peers marveled at his natural talent and reputed him as "a young genius." The genius of his work soon attracted the attention of rival cartoon studios interested in winning over the young cartoonist.

In 1920, a second turn of events would catapult Walter into a place of greater prominence to showcase his talent to the world. Pioneer animator J.R. Bray, who had opened a new studio, Bray Studios Incorporated, in 1914, with $10,000 in capital, brought Walter into the fold to work in his studio's art department after annexing the IFS films. At the time Hearst had closed his IFS studio, he had begun outsourcing the animation to other studios in New York to keep his comic-strip franchise "alive on screen." One of them was Bray's studio located on

26th Street in New York. Walter's hiring coincided that September with the departure of several disgruntled Bray staff members: Earl Hurd, Harry Bailey, and others. In June 1921, after fellow pioneer animator Max Fleischer left to open his own studio with his younger brother Dave, Bray appointed Walter "director general of Bray Productions," a position formerly held by Max Fleischer. Bray gave Walter as his first assignment the task of reviving his studio's most famous series, *Colonel Heeza Liar*. Bray had originally created the series to illustrate gags in magazines before using them in animation. Each cartoon followed the outlandish, hair-raising tales of the fibbing army colonel (inspired by President Teddy Roosevelt, known as a foremost teller of tales himself); hence the origin of his name.

Possibly the first true cartoon character to star in a long-term cartoon series, the Colonel originally starred in 39 cartoons from 1913 to 1917, produced by Bray for Pathé Film Exchange. In this updated second version, produced and directed by Vernon Stallings and animated by Walter (who also served as assistant director and writer), the Colonel interacted in the "live world" much like Max and Dave Fleischer's KoKo the Clown did in their famous live-action/animated cartoon shorts, *Out of the Inkwell*. The main attraction for audiences became the "special effects" of the bespectacled Colonel popping out of an inkwell, a device that "clearly intended to compete with the Fleischers'" successful *Out of the Inkwell* series.

The technique, which the Fleischers were the first to use, involved combining live footage of actors with animated drawings of characters in the same scene, often becoming an important thread to the story. In January 1923, a critic reviewing *Colonel Heeza Liar and the Ghost* noted how this technique was used to great effect: "A living actor, a Negro standing 5'10," shrinks until he is only half an inch in height. He is then transformed into a pair of dice which roll out of sight. Another living actor, six feet and heavy for his height, dives headlong into an ordinary waste basket."

Subsequent efforts used the inkwell motif in the opening live-action segment, once again for the purpose of establishing the story. In *Colonel Heeza Liar's Forbidden Fruit*, Walter appears on camera with

An early example of Lantz's hand-drawn artwork originally created for a trade advertisement promoting the *Goldwyn-Bray Comic* series in 1920.

another artist, engaged in an intense conversation at the animation table when the Colonel suddenly enters in the guise of a banana. Breaking from convention, the Colonel then pours the entire contents from the inkwell onto a sketchpad, on which begins his animated adventure.

Walter avoided topical ideas in coming up with stories for this new group of films. He believed if he observed this cardinal rule, a cartoon would play for years. As a result, he normally cast the Colonel in classic romps that spoofed everyday situations. The films, like most short subjects of their day, opened on the same bill with many other animated and live-action comedies. On February 26, 1923, for example, *Colonel Heeza Liar, Detective*—which *The New York Times* called "one of those skillful Bray cartoon comedies"—premiered at New York's Strand Theatre along with the split reel *Odds and Ends*; the Prizma color short *I Know a Garden*; and the Kinetico picture *Robert Louis Stevenson*, before Charlie Chaplin's silent comedy feature *The Pilgrim*.

In 1924, when Stallings, who also doubled as the studio's production manager, fell ill, Bray fired him after he directed his final *Colonel Heeza Liar* cartoon released that November and promoted Walter to chief animator. In making the move, he explained, "You now have the job; you write, you direct, you act. You can have one inker, one painter, one background artist and one cameraman." This served as Walter's indoctrination into the world of business as Bray believed that the cartoon business should be "run like any other." That year Bray made Walter the highest paid employee in the field of animation, paying him $250 a week. "In spite of his youth, Walt was one of the best animators in the business," noted animation legend James "Shamus" Culhane, who Walter hired in 1924 as an errand boy at "the magnificent salary" of $12 a week after looking over his drawings.

CHANGING COURSE

Later that year, as *Colonel Heeza Liar* had begun to run its course with audiences, Walter made a last impression by creating two new original characters for a new series. *Dinky Doodle* featured the misadventures of a meek, young boy dressed in a cloth cap and knickers (whom he modeled after the character in *Jerry on the Job*) and his faithful

Promotional still of J.R. Bray's teller of tall tales, Colonel Heeza Liar, with Lantz that he animated in a second round of silent cartoons for Bray starting in the early 1920s. *(Courtesy: Walter Lantz)*

bulbous-nosed dog, Weakheart, in cartoons with a heavy emphasis on "chases." Walter wrote, directed, and animated the series, along with his chief animators Clyde Geronimi and David Hand, who both later became key animators at Walt Disney Studios in the 1930s, and former Hearst *Daily Graphic* newspaper-sports-cartoonist-turned-animator Ving Fuller.

Walter made his directorial debut with the series that September of 1924, with the first entry, *The Magic Lamp*. The initial batch of films he made that year, a wonderful blend of live action with animation, were, as he put it, "burlesques on well-known fairy tales," including two others, *The Giant Killer* and *The Pied Piper*, animated in the same form as Paul Terry's *Aesop's Film Fables*, a popular curtain-raiser shown before the main attraction in movie theaters since 1920.

Between 1925 and 1926, as he later noted, Walter directed and scripted 26 additional films (only 23 titles from this period have been identified) in which he also acted in "live" situations in front of the camera, reminiscent of Fleischer's *Out of the Inkwell* cartoon shorts where the animator appeared on camera with the animated characters segueing into the actual cartoon. In the *Inkwell* films Fleischer typically sat behind an animator's table, bringing his hand-drawn sketches of the characters and picture's story to life in front of audiences' eyes. It was a stock opening that the famous pioneer animator used successfully for years. Walter's concept was unlike Fleischer's in that he did not always appear in the same location as Fleischer did, ensconced at his trusty animator's table. "We never opened a cartoon with the same setting. We went out to a field, and didn't just work at a desk like Fleischer did. Fleischer never left his office," Walter remembered. "We went outside to do our stories. We went to a beach or Buckhill Falls in upstate New York. We went all over."

Walter further distinguished himself from Fleischer by employing an entirely different process to seamlessly blend the live-action sequences with animation. Once the live-action scenes were shot, he took the negative and had 8-by-10 photographic stills made of every frame—some 3,000 to 4,000 altogether—for a single one-reel production. The stills were then methodically punched like animation paper and rephotographed with each cel of character animation overlapping the live-action scenes. The actual characters were drawn on onionskin paper, then inked and painted on clear acetate cels before being filmed in combination with the live-action enlargements.

Calling himself a "terrible actor" who had only "four expressions," Walter found acting in each film extremely difficult as he had to act without interacting with the characters or knowing how they were going to appear in each scene. As Culhane once recalled, "If Walt was supposed to duel a cartoon villain, he would first duel a live person, like Clyde Geronimi, one of his chief animators. The cartoon characters were added later and the final result was Walt dueling merrily with an animated cartoon."

The Bray studios produced more than just animated fare; its annual output included a bevy of live-action, educational slide-films (under a second company, Brayco) and two-reel comedies, which was one of the reasons why Walter left Hearst for Bray, to push the envelope in the medium. Recalling his sudden thrust into the acting world, Walter once said, "Stallings [who he replaced] often acted in the two-reel comedies Bray produced and I soon found I had to do the same. The first time I tried it I didn't know how to put make-up on."

The 25-year-old cartoonist acted as the comic lead in each film, starting with *Little Red Riding Hood*, released in January 1925. Like famous film comedians of the silent era, he got entangled in all kinds of mishaps with Dinky and Weakheart in their live-action and animated world. Discussing his role, Lantz once told the author, "I was short and not especially funny looking, so I imitated Harold Lloyd's prop eyeglasses. All the comedians of those days used something—Chaplin had his tramp outfit; Conklin a walrus moustache; Langdon that ill-fitting peaked cap. The glasses weren't too good a trademark for me, but then I wasn't aiming to be a full-time comedian."

The cost to produce these innovative and cutting-edge productions was $1,800 per one-reel short—a meager amount now, but a large expense in the 1920s. That was the total cost to produce 700 feet of live action and animation for a single cartoon. As Walter once confessed, "I had no idea what the cartoons were costing, so this figure didn't frighten me." Nonetheless he squeezed as much imagination as possible out of every foot of film. Unfortunately most of these silent gems were tragically destroyed in a warehouse fire some years back, leaving behind little evidence of their creation and innovation. The few existing films, however, give credence to the belief that silent cartoons represented some of Walter's finest work.

Walter's *Dinky Doodle* series became so popular with filmgoers and exhibitors that nearly every new installment premiered at the Capitol Theatre in New York. The fairy-tale versions, of course, drew big laughs, as did the classic romps, both styles proving to be highly entertaining.

Lantz brings to life on the drawing board his original creations, Dinky Doodle and Weakheart, stars of their own live-action/animated series, which he animated and directed and in which he co-starred. *(Courtesy: Walter Lantz)*

Lantz is up to his neck in trouble in this scene from his popular combination live-action/animated series *Dinky Doodle*. *(Courtesy: Walter Lantz)*

Never one to pick favorites in his career, Walter once pointed out during an interview, however, two films he considered as popular examples. The first was *Dinky Doodle in the Hunt*. Arriving in theaters on November 1, 1925, the black-and-white short plays like a slapstick comedy of the era, with Walter, in live footage, being chased by a cartoon bear during a hunting trip gone amuck. When the bear draws closer, Walter springs forward, barely eluding the big bad grizzly. His second choice was *Dinky Doodle in Egypt* (1926), this time with Walter as the famed Egyptian queen, Cleopatra, in drag.

Overall, Walt found producing the *Dinky Doodle* cartoons a worthwhile experience, more so than *Colonel Heeza Liar*. "I enjoyed the series, naturally because I created it and felt closer to the characters," he once explained. "Not only that, but Colonel Heeza Liar was one of these Baron Munchausen types where he does nothing but tell a big fib. After a while that grew old." (Baron Munchausen was a character Jack Pearl played on his NBC radio show in the 1930s. He coined the popular catchphrase, "Vas you dere, Sharlie?")

SHAKING UP HISTORY

Overlapping the second year of *Dinky Doodle* was Walter's newest creation and third cartoon series for Bray, *Un-Natural History* (billed in movie posters as "An Un-Natural History Comedy"). This series featured outlandish history fables blending live-action and animation as animated by Clyde Geronimi and David Hand, who later co-directed some films with Lantz in 1926, and animator Earl Hurd, who returned to Bray in 1925 after efforts to launch his Kew Gardens studio failed. From its inaugural year through September 1926, the films alternated in rotation with Walter's *Dinky Doodle* cartoons and were distributed by Film Booking Offices of America (FBO). Series titles, beginning with the first released in October 1925, included *How the Elephant Got His Trunk*, *How the Bear Got His Short Tail*, *How the Camel Got His Hump*, and *The Leopard's Spots*.

Unlike *Dinky Doodle*, in which he was the lone actor in the films, Walter contracted child actors to play in live-action/animated scenes

Original poster for the 1926 Dinky Doodle cartoon *Dinky Doodle in The Arctic.*

opposite animated characters, to tell the stories that often involved a deep moral of some kind. One such child actor to star in the films was actress Anita Louise, who later became a famous contract player at 20th Century Fox.

The following year, in 1926, while simultaneously writing and directing *Dinky Doodle* (and also starring in it) and *Un-Natural History*, both their final years in release, Walter created and directed his fourth and final cartoon series for Bray, *Pete the Pup*. Billed in ads and posters under the name *Hot Dog Cartoons*, this latest creation cast a lovable but pesky pup and jocular tramp sidekick in funny misadventures.

While reportedly modeling Pete after KoKo the Clown's new sidekick, Fritz the dog, in Fleischer's *Out of the Inkwell* films, Lantz was not nearly as forthcoming about what prompted him to spawn Pete. As he explained, "You create them. You really don't know why you create these characters. No one had ever done a dog and a boy. The same went for Woody Woodpecker. No one had animated a woodpecker, or a panda, or a walrus, or a buzzard. I always tried to pick something that hadn't been done."

First starring in *For the Love O' Pete*, released on October 2, 1926, the films relied heavily on Fleischer's *Out of the Inkwell* technique blending live-action sequences of Walter as a "dapper artist" and as directed by Geronimi with animation of his cartoon pup to open each story. While lasting only six months, *Pete the Pup* (also known as *Hot Dog Cartoons*) is rated by many historians as Walter's best technical work during this period.

Of films that survived from this time, Walter deemed two films as good representations of the series as a whole. One of them was *Lunch Hound*. Opening in theaters on April 23, 1927, this silent cartoon short begins with Walter at the drawing table drawing a roast turkey to "entice his pup out of hiding." The little pup (reminiscent of Weakheart in the *Dinky Doodle* cartoons), drawn out of a grove of trees by such a tantalizing temptation, interacts with Walter, cutting back and forth between live-action and animation. The complex process was orchestrated by James "Shamus" Culhane. After working summers at the studio first as an errand boy, then as a plot man, opaquer, and darkroom assistant, Culhane was responsible for producing the combined shots in this and many other cartoon shorts made by the studio that decade.

Another classic romp Walter handpicked as displaying his razor-sharp writing and slapstick humor was *Bone Dry*. Released to movie houses on May 14, 1927, this funny fish tale has Weakheart fishing and catching a fish in a "live" pond while Walter fishes in a cartoon lake and winds up with a cartoon fish. In one scene he comically baits his hook, using animated worms, and in the background can be seen live footage of real animals in the forest. The cartoon makes good use of combining live and animated footage.

Later assessing Walter's originality, innovativeness, and overall contributions as an animator and director, author Donald Crafton in his history of silent animated cartoons, *Before Mickey: The Animated Film 1898–1928*, wrote that although his films were not "very innovative . . . during this formative period his technical skill and his organizational capacity were evident and maturing. The films had a youthful verve and devil-may-care quality that would not always be found at the Lantz Studio when it became one of the most important ones of the 1930s and 1940s."

Walter truly turned out magnificent work despite the adversity of tight budgets and employing a small animation crew of about seven people, including his assistant Clyde Geronimi, an inker, a painter, background artists, and a cameraman. Wearing multiple hats, he performed the writing and directing and animating of most every cartoon besides starring in them. (During his time at Bray, Walter was also featured as a comedy star with Tiny Ward and Marny Shaw in the live-action silent comedy two-reeler, *Barnyard Rivals*, which was released in 1928.)

Pete the Pup and *Un-Natural History* remained in production until the Bray Studios shut down in 1927. There was not much money left in silent cartoons anymore. Sound was in the offing, and competition was becoming stiff. Bray just could not challenge his larger, more powerful opponents much longer, so he decided to cease operation of his cartoon department completely. That put his staff of seven—including Lantz—out of work. With no other positions to be found in the New York area, Walter contemplated his future. The climate for cartoons,

Overlapping with the second year of production of Lantz's *Dinky Doodle* cartoons was his series of outlandish historical fables blending live-action and animation, *Un-Natural History*, whose releases included 1926's *The Pig's Curly Tail*. (Courtesy: Walter Lantz)

Poster promoting Lantz's 1926 creation, the pesky Pete the Pup, of *Hot Dog Cartoons* series fame, including *S'Matter Pete*. *(Courtesy: Walter Lantz)*

wrote Shamus Culhane in his autobiography, *Talking Animals and Other People*, "sunk so low that audiences booed and hissed when the main title of a cartoon came on the screen." As Culhane added, "Walter gave me my back pay and a letter of recommendation . . . and was going to leave the animation business."

After seven years at Bray, what Walter planned to do next soon unfolded, taking him on a remarkable journey that would end with him staking his own claim as a Hollywood animator.

3

Staking His
Claim Out West

In 1927, with the cartoon industry in the midst of a serious "slump," Walter's future looked dim at that moment. Theater bookings were in decline, resulting in a severe drop in rental rates or revenue for all the major cartoon studios. Many artists were forced to leave the profession and go back to drawing newspaper comic strips for a living. After reaching the pinnacle of success, it appeared as though the industry was ready to collapse as many studios, including Walter's employer, the Bray Studios, struggled to survive. Although Walter was widely recognized for writing and directing his cartoons, he could sense that the prospects for staying in the profession on the East Coast appeared grim.

Around this time Hollywood was on the threshold of becoming the new entertainment capital of the world for both live-action films and animation. Producers were discovering the benefits of making films on the West Coast, where the only other "Walt" in the business, Walt Disney, had established his own studio and was producing a series of *Oswald the Lucky Rabbit* cartoons for Carl Laemmle's Universal Pictures. Not long after, others followed suit and set up shop to produce cartoons almost entirely on the West Coast. Walter confided in his father, Frank, about the state of the industry and his desire to head west to Hollywood to seize other opportunities. Realizing the tremendous career and

36

financial upsides such a move would offer his talented son, he simply said, "Go."

From his time with Bray Studios, Walter was fortunate to have saved $10,000.

With that money he bought himself a brand-new Locomobile, a brand of automobiles that became known for its line of well-built and speedy luxury cars. Throwing all caution to the wind and letting destiny be his guide, he packed his belongings and drove to California. The day he arrived, he secured a room at the Hollywood Athletic Club, which just happened to be next to one occupied by Frank Capra. The Sicilian-born auteur would become a life-long friend of Walter's and, more importantly, one of the most popular American film directors of all time. After breaking in as a gag writer in 1924 on Hal Roach's *Our Gang* comedies, Capra then became a writer-director for pioneer comedy filmmaker Mack Sennett before cowriting a series of increasingly popular comedy shorts and directing three feature films starring baby-faced comedian Harry Langdon at the peak of his career. Also on the day Walter arrived, he immediately got his first taste of Hollywood living when his friend Bob Vignola invited him to a star-studded bash in honor of Belle Baker, featuring many of the major movers and shakers in the business on hand, including comedian Buster Keaton, actress Gloria Swanson, producer Irving Thalberg, and singer Sophie Tucker.

Becoming perhaps better known for his on-camera antics as a lead comic in his cartoons than for his animation, Walter's brush with Hollywood filmmaking took him down an unexpected path. He starred in a series of two-reel, live-action comedies for his former employer J.R. Bray, who had established a West Coast production office at Larry Darmoor's studios in Hollywood and put Walter to work. In a short time, Walter felt like a fish out of water not doing what he truly loved: animation. As he told Bray, "I don't like this. I want to go back to animation."

Walter met with Disney, approaching him about working for his studio. But the young animator but did not need another writer, director, or producer; he needed only animators, which would have been a step down for Walter in both prestige and pay given his higher ranking in the business.

Instead Walter went to work for a producer he met at one of Vignola's celebrity bashes: Sam Van Ronkel. Producing the two-reel, comedy series *Andy Gump*, based on the popular daily newspaper comic strip for Universal Pictures, Van Ronkel was seeking an animator to dispense his "magic touch" on his obscure, low-budget productions. He hired Walter as a story man and animation gag man. Walter worked for several weeks with Ronkel and his production crew, helping them concoct the screwball madness that occurred on the screen and iron out some of the complex technical issues in making the films.

Remembering those days, Walter related in an interview, "I came out to Universal and made a few animated shots on the *Andy Gump* series. One, for instance, had Andy dreaming that he was going to the moon. I showed him asleep. While he was asleep, I made his mattress take off with him out the window off to the moon. That's how I became known at Universal."

WORKING WITH THE MASTERS OF COMEDY

Like his previous situation with Bray, however, Walter quickly grew restless and was ready to jump ship as his chances for advancements were slim because Universal was not willing to pay "top salaries for top talent." Destiny intervened once again when Van Ronkel introduced the ambitious young animator to Leo McCarey, the former Hal Roach and Mack Sennett comedy film director with whom Walter developed an instant camaraderie. Like Walter, McCarey had previously worked as a gag man for Roach on his *Our Gang* series. He then produced and directed two-reel comedies with comedian Charley Chase and was responsible for casting and guiding the development of two comedians, Stan Laurel and Oliver Hardy, in what would become one of the most enduring comedy teams of all time, known as Laurel and Hardy. Walter enjoyed his conversations so much with the handsome comedy helmsman that he wanted to go to work for him, but McCarey told him straight up, "Walter, I'd love to have you, but our staff is filled and I can't pay you anything."

Taking a great risk, Walter countered, "I don't want the money. I have money. I'll work for nothing, just so I can sit in and see how you work. I'd like to get some experience on two-reel comedies."

Walter got his wish. McCarey took him under his wing, paying him nothing in exchange for giving him the experience he wanted. Walter watched as the comedy master McCarey worked his magic on the sets and sound stages of the Hal Roach Studios in Culver City, California, filming and creating some of the most beloved live-action comedy two-reelers of the silent and sound eras. He was in lockstep with McCarey as he supervised the bumbling Stan Laurel and comically annoyed Oliver Hardy in their classic films and shot routines. Walter simply scripted on sheets of paper without an actual shooting script, learning everything he wanted about making two-reel comedies in the process. As Walter told biographer Joe Adamson, "I didn't know what a gag was until I came to Hollywood—never heard the word. I made hundreds of cartoons back east, but these were birds-and-bees stories, cute little fairy tales. I learned about gags from the two-reel producers and directors and actors, just by watching and listening."

Walter put his artistic abilities and comic sense to work on films McCarey directed by storyboarding—a series of sketches he drew—the comedy that appeared on screen. In no time people started putting two-and-two together that he was the same man responsible for inventing those wildly hilarious cartoons made in New York. Walter created several onscreen gags for Laurel and Hardy comedies. One of them involved musical notes emerging out of the horn-shaped speaker of an old Victrola (a turntable for phonographs or records built into a wooden cabinet) and dancing on the noses of the comedians, rousing them out of a deep sleep. For the 1928 Stone Age romp, *Flying Elephants*, filmed in mid-May 1927, and featuring Laurel and Hardy as costumed cavemen, Walter dreamed up the memorable animation of three pachyderms flying south, following Hardy's comical setup line, "Beautiful weather—the elephants are flying south."

Walter's stay at Roach Studios was short-lived, only six weeks. Destiny called him elsewhere, this time to the Mack Sennett studio. Pinto Colvig, later to gain fame as the voice of Disney cartoon stars Goofy, Grumpy, and Sleepy, was hard at work as a gag man for Sennett. Dubbed the "King of Comedy" for producing slapstick comedies noted for their wild car chases and custard pie warfare, Sennett needed someone of Walter's expertise to animate a giant cootie in one scene of his latest feature film *The Good-Bye Kiss* (1928).

Of Sennett's dilemma, Walter told the author in an interview: "Mr. Sennett had a problem. He was doing a feature film and wanted to show a cootie. A cootie was a bug that got into the uniforms of soldiers during the First World War. In this picture, Sennett had a scene where all these soldiers are in the trenches and all of a sudden there comes along a cootie [going across the battflefield]. A tremendous cootie—just gigantic—who scares all the soldiers so much that they jump out of the trenches and head for the horizon. Sennett had had several animators try to animate the cootie, but nobody could do it."

Realizing that Walter had the skill and "know-how" to do the job, Colvig instantly recommended him to the entrepreneur filmmaker, known to his crew as "Old Man" for his typically crusty and irascible demeanor. Upon their first meeting, Sennett asked Walter if he could do the scene. Walter replied, "Just give me the film of the scared soldiers, and on cue having them throwing up their rifles and running off into the distance."

Given his experience with previous animators unable to deliver what he wanted, Sennett looked at Walter dubiously before giving him the okay. Walter took the film footage of the soldiers and animated the cootie, which, as he described, was "just a black dot with six legs walking across the screen." It took him 50 drawings and one afternoon to complete. He subsequently built the gag up more in the scene with the captain spotting the cootie through his binoculars and then the cootie climbing on the frame of the binoculars and "going up one side, sliding down the other."

Sennett's optical department crew then superimposed the footage of Walter's cartoon cootie over the shot of the soldiers, which they processed and finished in about a week. Walter was so proud of the end result he ran the finished footage for Sennett's gag men, who advised him to "hold off" showing it to Sennett for about three weeks. "You could draw your salary here, and you wouldn't have to do anything but sit around and listen in on the story department," they said. "If he thought you had done what he wanted in such a short time, he wouldn't appreciate it as much."

Not privy to Sennett's complex personality firsthand after being on the payroll only a short time, Walter heeded their sage advice. He waited exactly three weeks. Then he gathered everyone around in the projection room with Sennett and showed him the end result. Sennett, a habitual tobacco chewer, watched the few seconds of footage unfold on the screen in front of him, alternately spitting chew into a sandbox and howling with laughter. Afterward, the delighted director slapped Walter on his thigh and said, "Lantz, you're in. I'm going to give you a job here."

Walter got to work and hung around with Sennett's story men, who concocted every kind of cartoon gag they could think of to make the most of his talent as an animator. For some six months he worked at the famous comedy film factory as a gag man, writer, and animator, and was fortunate to be "at the right place, at the right time." As Walter later revealed, "I didn't know what slapstick was until I came out here and worked for Mack Sennett. Then I realized it took pratfalls and socks on the head and being shot at to get big laughs in the theatre. The pies in the face, and so forth."

Things suddenly changed, however. Around Christmas 1927, Walter looked on as many of his colleagues in the story department and other production units were pink-slipped and laid off before the approaching holidays. That is, everyone but Walter.

Even then, his future with the studio was tenuous. As he started thinking he was "the fair-haired boy" of the studio, Sennett called him into his office before Christmas and between spitting streams of tobacco juice into a nearby spittoon said, "Lantz, you're a nice kid, and I like the work you've done for us. You're new out here, and I didn't want to embarrass you too much, so I kept you to last. I won't need you any-more. The studio is closing down and won't open up again till March."

At a party on New Year's Eve 1927, thrown by his friend Bob Vignola at his posh villa following an afternoon of playing cards by Walter, Vignola, and actor George Duryea (later known as Tom Keene and Richard Powers), Walter would meet for the first time a beautiful young stage actress. She had come into town from a two-year Australian tour of *Abie's Irish Rose*. She was the New York–born Grace Stafford (nee Boyle). The chemistry that developed between Walter and her was immediate, and they saw each other many times after that first meeting but dated and married other people. Stafford married Duryea in the late 1920s, while Walter, after courting the dark-haired and dark-eyed beauty, who was seven years younger than him, Ethel Doris Hollister, the daughter of pioneer American cinematographer George K. Hollister, took the plunge a few years later. Like Walter, Doris originally hailed from New York. Growing up in the Bronx with her younger brother, George, she and her family moved to Los Angeles around 1920.

LUCKING OUT WITH A RABBIT

Walter hung around Hollywood, hoping to find employment. In the meantime circumstances already set into motion would soon land him elsewhere. The "other Walt" in the business, Walt Disney, was losing a character his studio had been animating and directing in a series of theatrical cartoon shorts, called *Oswald the Lucky Rabbit*. In early February 1928, the matter reached a boiling point after Disney requested a raise for renewal of his contract with producer Charles Mintz and his brother-in-law George Winkler of Winkler Pictures, which distributed the films to theaters. After Disney refused to accept their counteroffer, they awarded the rights to *Oswald* to Universal Pictures with ex-Disney animators Hugh Harman, Rollin "R.C." Hamilton, Paul Smith, and Ben Clopton completing work on the remaining *Oswald* cartoons for Disney before joining Mintz's new studio to produce their own new series in early May of that year.

Meanwhile Disney ended up financing a character he had created and animator Ub Iwerks had designed, a little mouse they called Mickey that ultimately made Disney "king of the cartoon world." Universal Studios's whole sales department rejected the idea. As Walter later related, "What did they want with another mouse after all the mice drawn by Paul Terry?" Disney then found a home for his character at Columbia Pictures, which distributed the series and became a wild success.

Walter was among a handful of new recruits to join Mintz's studio as well, including Isadore "Friz" Freleng, who Disney had fired

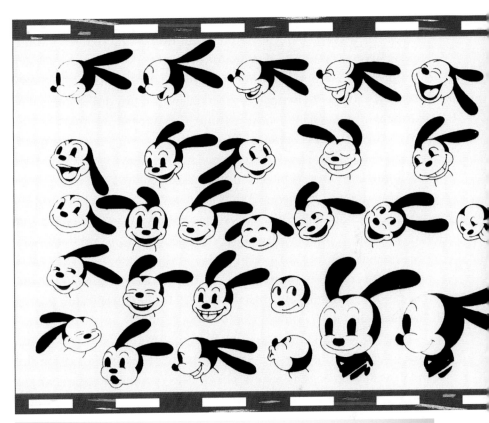

Model sheet for Lantz's modified version of Walt Disney's *Oswald the Lucky Rabbit* from after Lantz took over the character. The character starred in 195 cartoons for his studio. *(Courtesy: Walter Lantz)*

over "creative differences" several months earlier; Manuel Moreno, Ray Abrams, and former Mack Sennett gag man Pinto Colvig as inbetweeners (those who draw in-between or transition drawings in an animated scene); and Fred "Tex" Avery, who later became a legendary screwball cartoon director at Warner Bros. and MGM. Winkler's crew produced their films at a ramshackle studio on the Universal lot. The place was so old that, according to Walter, when he first started, he had to hold an umbrella over his drawing board when it rained.

In 1928, the Winkler Studio produced nine *Oswald* cartoons during its first year of operation. As a whole, the low-budget cartoons were not markedly different from Walt Disney's. The films featured some of Disney's same crude barnyard humor and Iwerks's mechanical humor. Nonetheless, all were fairly successful.

The first *Oswald* they produced, *High Up*, made its theatrical debut on July 23, 1928. Walter served uncredited as a director of the series, starting with *Mississippi Mud*, the studio's second release that year. He received his first onscreen credit after codirecting with Tom Palmer the seventh *Oswald* cartoon, *Bull-Oney*, released to theaters in late November. In the film, Oswald meets his match as a bull trainer trying to get an underweight bull into shape; he manages to lure the bull into the ring, but the bull makes his getaway in the end. Walter codirected with R.C. Hamilton another Oswald short—the final one produced and released that year on Christmas Eve day—called *Farmyard Follies*. Composed of a series of barnyard antics, this time Oswald mixes it up with a sassy young hen after she mistakes his tail for her quarry after a worm she wants disappears down a hole. The two tangle and Oswald fares no better at washing a tiny pig in a washtub or milking a cow when a pack of flies wearing skates decides to use her back like a skating rink and Oswald's nose as a "resting place." The young hen returns to give Oswald more trouble, forcing him to take an axe and chop her head off, but the now headless hen refuses to give up and challenges him to a "free-for-all."

The following year, in 1929, after Walt Disney transformed the industry by breaking the "sound barrier" with the release of *Steamboat Willie*, Walter directed and codirected three additional *Oswald* cartoons under the Winkler Studios banner. That year Winkler and Mintz produced and released 17 new *Oswald* cartoons in optional synchronized sound and musical scores (as provided by Bert Fiske) and silent prints, starting with *Hen Fruit*, as a way to "catch up" with Disney. For the musical accompaniment and synchronization, Winkler's staff employed a "pots and pans" method of creating sound effects. As Walter once recalled, "It was funny how we did it. We had a bench with all the props on it—the bells, and so on. And we'd project a cartoon on the screen and all of us would stand there in front of the cartoon. As the action progressed, we'd take it and make sound effects, dialogue, and all. We never pre-scored these films. We did everything as we watched the picture. It was the only way we knew how to add sound." In each short, Oswald's voice was created by a slide whistle.

On January 21, 1929, Walter's latest *Oswald* short hit movie theaters, *Yanky Clippers* (incorrectly titled in some sources as *Yankee Clippers*). Codirected by Tom Palmer, this comical romp follows Oswald's misadventures as a barber shop owner whose "animated barber pole seizes prospective customers, willing or not, and shoots them through the roof into the barber's chair." Oswald also encounters a lascivious wolf (Pete) who falls hard for Oswald, who is disguised as a female manicurist, while waiting impatiently for a manicure.

Nearly four months lapsed before audiences were treated to the further antics of Oswald the Lucky Rabbit under Walter's direction. On May 13, he solely helmed his second synchronized sound and scored cartoon that year, *Stage Stunts*. In his latest foray, Oswald makes his stage acting debut as a snake charmer and xylophone player until a mean audience member breaks his instrument into pieces. Undeterred, Oswald picks up where he left off, using a skinny horse's ribs as a makeshift instrument on which to play music and entertain the audience. However, after a pup tosses a bomb that the horse swallows, panic breaks out as members of the audience make a mad dash for the exits before the bomb goes off and Oswald pokes his head inside the horse's mouth. Oswald is asleep the whole time. He awakens to think he had a "pleasant dream" of kissing a nymph, only to find himself lip-locked for real with the horse. Afterward he has the horse clobber him on the head and knock him out so he can return to dreaming.

On May 27, exactly two weeks later, Walter entertained audiences with his third directorial effort starring Oswald, *Stripes and Stars*. After every available cop is blown up trying to catch a gangster and jewel thief, Big Bruin Boloney, Oswald is promoted to cop as their last resort. He becomes an unlikely hero after capturing the big bad bear and is made into a judge for his efforts. The film became a notable effort on Walter's part, with critic Raymond Ganley in *Motion Picture News* writing in his May 11, 1929, review: "Sound lifts this Oswald, just about an average cartoon, into the laugh realm and makes of it a bright reel that'll liven up programs handicapped by deadwood features. The rabbit is a porter delegated to capture a lawbreaking bear terrorizing the police force. He gets his man and hauls him before his chief to collect the reward of judgeship. Several really good ideas, the work of the nimble-witted cartoonists, decorate the affair and push it along to a laugh *finis*. Walter Lantz, billed as the director, is probably chiefly responsible for its success."

Meanwhile Winkler's operation began to show signs of unraveling. Two of his staffers, Hugh Harman and Rudolph Ising, offered to Universal to produce the Oswald cartoons themselves and "edge out Mintz in the same manner as he had previously done to Disney." At the same time, they were producing an additional cartoon series with sound, *Bosko the Talk-Ink Kid*, starring their own black-faced creation, which they later produced for Warner Bros. instead. Universal rejected their proposal. Studio founder Carl Laemmle Sr. (known as "Uncle Carl" to his employees) had grown tired of "all the shuffling around" involved in contracting an outside animation studio. He terminated the Winkler-Mintz contract and decided to establish his own cartoon department, originally called Universal Studio Cartoons, to produce the Oswald cartoon series directly on the studio lot instead. The man he put in charge of that effort was Walter Lantz, awarding him a seven-year contract. As Walter remembered in an interview with the author, "Mr. Laemmle asked me if I would set up a cartoon department for them . . . So I had to rebuild. They gave me a big sound stage and we converted it into a cartoon department, later adding desks, drawing boards, cameras, and a good staff of animators. I got a lot of animators I knew from New York to come out here and work for me."

Some historians have speculated that Walter was "actively involved in Laemmle's decision," with a primary interest in controlling the rights to Oswald, something that was unattainable in the Mintz-Winkler studio. That year, while "schmoozing" with Laemmle, Walter actually won the rights to Oswald and the studio after winning both in a poker game with the famed movie mogul.

Walter was enthusiastic over the opportunity to run his own studio. To compete with other more established cartoon studios, including Disney, he initially staffed his animation corps with former Disney

Full-color poster for Lantz's ninth Oswald the Lucky Rabbit cartoon he produced and directed in synchronized sound under his studio for Universal in 1929, *Nutty Notes. (Courtesy: Walter Lantz)*

animators—people like Hugh Harman, Rudolf Ising, and Friz Freleng, who later made his mark at Warner Bros. Some new staffers came and went rather quickly. Ex-Winkler staffers Tom Palmer and R.C. Hamilton jumped over to Disney and Harman-Ising in early 1930, respectively. Colvig departed for Disney in 1931, making a name for himself as a studio gag man and voice artist. Former Winkler musical director Bert Fiske stayed at the helm until he left the studio in September 1929, and was replaced by Dutch composer David Broekman, who was perhaps best known for his musical scores on such Universal features as the 1930 Academy Award winner *All Quiet on the Western Front*.

By the time Walter started producing the Oswald shorts, he had 120 people on staff under his authority, and the atmosphere at his studio was much more casual than others. He knew everyone by their first name, and they all simply called him "Walter." Remarkably, by the time he was 30, he had already worked as a manager, director, and producer of his own cartoons and for "one of the biggest studios in the business." One of his wisest decisions in building his studio was to hire Irish-American animator Bill Nolan, who created the "rubber hose" style of animation and was responsible for streamlining the design of Felix the Cat. A huge advantage Walter had in hiring him over Disney, who likewise recruited him after he left Mintz's New York Krazy Kat studio, was that he and Nolan had previously worked together in New York and were friends. Along with Nolan, Walter brought on board many young and creative artists who would be responsible for giving his studio its "unique character," including Manuel Moreno, Tex Avery, Ray Abrams, Clyde Geronomi, La Verne Harding, Sid Sutherland, Virgil Ross, Fred Kopietz, and Lester Kline, all of whom started out as inbetweeners.

When Walter took over the Oswald series, he decided to make many dramatic changes in the famed rabbit's appearance. He redesigned the character by brightening him up from his typically black drawing style that Disney's and Mintz's animators had used. As Walter stated in an interview with the author, "The Disney stories were great, mind you . . . very funny. But I didn't like the rabbit. He was just black-and-white. He wouldn't have any appeal for commercial items like comic books, or that sort of thing. So I took it on because if I could change the rabbit I would do it."

As a result, he made Oswald more "cute" in nature, a natural white rabbit that people often found in children's books. That metamorphosis gave Oswald a certain ray of charm that not even the original Disney character provided.

The Fishing Fool (1929) was the last Mintz-Winkler *Oswald* cartoon. Walter and his new team of animators immediately began producing a handful of cartoons later that year, starting with *Race Riot*, his studio's first release through Universal. Premiering on September 2, 1929, the film, along with other 1929 releases, featured set plots and stories much like the earlier Disney and Winkler shorts. Walter was aware that the series had room for improvement, finding the initial stories inhibiting and the animation not up to his standards. As a result, he worked closely with his animation staff to smooth out the "rough edges," largely evident in future releases.

MAKING CARTOON HISTORY

Laemmle asked Walter, between running and launching his new studio, to contribute an animated segment for the studio's all-talking extravaganza, *King of Jazz*, starring Paul Whiteman and his band. The film was announced as a musical revue along the lines of a vaudeville or stage production. In late October 1929, Whiteman and his group left New York by train for Los Angeles; filming commenced shortly after their arrival and the completion of the script.

King of Jazz was to become the second all-talking motion picture filmed entirely in two-color Technicolor, not just color sequences (the first-ever, all-talking, all color, feature-length movie was the 1929 Warner Bros. film *On With the Show*), and the first to use a prerecorded soundtrack produced separately from the actual filming. Whiteman insisted that the movie's entire soundtrack be prerecorded to obtain the "best sound" quality and to avoid poor recording conditions and extraneous noises common in a movie studio setting. After Universal opposed the idea, they reluctantly relented and only after the sound was recorded were the scenes filmed and then later synchronized with the soundtrack. The movie was originally budgeted at $1.5 million to produce. Due to long delays in developing an acceptable script, the cost of salaries and living quarters for Whiteman and his band, the expensive sets that were built and subsequently demolished and never used, and the lavish cost of the production itself, the film ended up costing almost $2 million. The movie, upon its release, was originally 105 minutes long. Later it was shortened to 93 minutes, with three sequences being cut for all re-releases after Hollywood's Production Code went into effect in July 1934.

King of Jazz was historically significant another way: The animated segment Walter produced for the film became the first two-color Technicolor animation released in the sound era, predating Walt Disney and Ub Iwerks, a distinction that no other animator could claim. Iwerks animated and released his first *Flip the Frog* cartoon, *Fiddlesticks,* in two-strip Cinecolor, later that year. In 1933, Disney championed the use of three-strip Technicolor exclusively starting with his *Silly Symphony* cartoon *Three Little Pigs.*

Walter teamed up with director Bill Nolan and his animation staff to animate the sequence—and ostensibly the brightest moment in the film—of the famous bandleader Whiteman as a big-game hunter, hunting in Africa. He is chased by a lion, which he suddenly tames by playing the soothing song "Music Hath Charms" on his violin. In the course of all the commotion, a monkey tosses a coconut at an elephant that squirts water at him, intending to hit the pachyderm but instead conking Whiteman on the head. The blow creates a bump that mushrooms into a crown, whereupon Whiteman is appropriately crowned "King of Jazz." Making a brief cameo appearance is Walter's Oswald the Lucky Rabbit, who takes part in some hilarious antics menacing other characters in the sequence.

Whiteman provided his own voice for his mustachioed alter ego. The young and talented crooner Bing Crosby, then a member of the Rhythm Boys, along with singers Harry Barris and Al Rinker who worked in Whiteman's band, created the vocal characterization and singing voice of the lion. Crosby recorded his vocal tracks and singing of other popular tunes, such as "So the Bluebirds and the Blackbirds Got Together," "A Bench in the Park," and "Happy Feet," in film right on the Universal lot. Featured throughout the segment were numerous 17th-, 18th-, and 19th-century classical songs, among them, "For He's a Jolly Good Fellow," the "Hunt Theme" (also known as "A-Hunting We Will Go"), "Tantivy, My Boys, Tantivy," "The Whistler and His Dog," and others, all arranged by Walter's latest staff addition, his new musical director James "Jimmy" Dietrich. He would score the bulwark of *Oswald* films for Walter's studio in the late 1930s, besides adding scores to Disney's silent *Oswald* cartoons that were later reissued with sound.

It is believed to have been the first time Crosby recorded a song for a motion picture. Walter owed Whiteman credit for a brilliant stroke of casting. When he told the conductor that the scene called for a lion singing a chorus of music, Whiteman reportedly enthused, "How about that kid Crosby?"

"I guess he'd be all right," Walter replied.

In doing the cartoon segment in Technicolor, however, Walter and his staff of artists and animators ran into unexpected difficulties in its production. First, since the film and cartoon were both being filmed using a two-strip color process, the range of colors were limited to mostly red and green. Likewise, artists found the paints they used to paint each animated cartoon cel would not adhere to it and often chipped off before the cels could be filmed or photographed. Despite these setbacks, Walter prevailed and delivered precisely what Laemmle had ordered.

The film was not without controversy, however. In November 1929, after filming had begun, Crosby was involved in major a automobile collision, resulting in serious injury to the passenger in his car. The young singer and the other driver were both booked for reckless and drunken driving during Prohibition, when the sale and distribution of alcohol was against the law, and the judge sentenced him to 60 days in jail. Crosby served only around 40 days of his sentence before he was released and, during his sentence after special arrangements were made, a policeman escorted him to and from the studio for filming so production could continue without further interruption. (Due to his sentencing, he lost the lead singing role in the "Song of the Dawn" production number to John Boles.)

The film's premiere on April 20, 1930, at Los Angeles's Criterion Theater two weeks before its grand premiere at the Roxy Theater in New York, included a stage show featuring Whiteman and his band and the legendary George Gershwin. *King of Jazz* was released to theaters nationwide on August 17, 1930, a day after Metro-Goldwyn-Mayer released Iwerks's first two-strip Cinecolor *Flip the Frog* cartoon, *Fiddlesticks*. On June 20, two months after the *King of Jazz's* Los Angeles debut, Universal also released a black-and-white *Oswald* cartoon Walter had directed, *My Pal Paul*, to help promote the feature and which included songs from the movie and featured Whiteman in cartoon form.

Produced by Laemmle's son, Carl Laemmle Jr. (whom his father appointed as head of the studio on his 21st birthday in 1928) and directed by John Murray Anderson, the costly feature-length musical fared poorly, losing an enormous amount of money for Universal. The movie made less than $900,000 and was subsequently dubbed "Universal's Rhapsody in the Red." Overseas, the movie performed better, especially in Cape Town, South Africa, where it played for 17 return engagements and eventually made a profit. Unfortunately, following countless delays, by the time the movie hit movie theaters in the United States, audiences had grown tired of movie musicals starting with the 1929 film *Broadway Melody*. In addition, the economic downturn of the Depression also prevented the movie from enjoying a more successful run, with many people electing to spend money only on the essentials. Even so, later that year, *King of Jazz* was awarded an Oscar for "Best Art Director," the only category in which the film was nominated, for the work of its Dutch-born art director Herman Rosse.

Critics were ebullient about Walter's effort at the first sound color cartoon. Believing his cartoon segment stole the show, a critic for the *Motion Picture Herald* wrote: "'The King of Jazz Revue' is a symphony of color and music with a blending of comedy, sensational settings, and intimate numbers to make the production commanding entertainment...From the animated color cartoon at the start, showing a comedy conception of how Whiteman was crowned King of Jazz through the stupendous 'Melting Pot' finale, the all Technicolor production is packed with genuine entertainment."

Being *first* was something for which Walter was extremely proud, and he was especially pleased by the reaction of moviegoers in theaters where the movie opened. As he remembered, "They had never seen anything like that before. It was the first two-strip color cartoon, and Bill Nolan and quite a few others did the animation, along with myself. It was just a terrific vehicle!"

In 1930, Walter's studio also produced a record high 24 *Oswald the Lucky Rabbit* cartoons, including Walter's last-credited film as an animator, which he also directed that May, *Tramping Tramps*. The average budget for an *Oswald* cartoon was around $4,000 a film. That was not as much as other producers were spending, but the reason for these low budgets was Walter was a budget-conscious director. He knew how to run a tight budget for each cartoon—squeezing as much quality as possible from each dollar.

As his studio expanded along with the number of films he produced, Walter made Nolan codirector and head animator of the studio to relieve unwanted pressures and demands on his time. The two men worked well together and produced a series of markedly and consistently funnier *Oswald* cartoons. The new *Oswald* cartoons were fundamentally different after Walter hired Jimmy Dietrich, who stayed on until 1937, to replace David Broekman as his musical director. The films became more like 1920s jazz-era musicals, with stories made up for a series of gags wrapped around a simple premise. Nolan became a major influence. He brought his brand of New York–style animation and humor that was "wild, boozy, unpredictable, and fundamentally abstract" and punctuated by "the most outrageous gags" to the *Oswald* cartoons he codirected with Walter. The first cartoon, *The Singing Sap*, was released in September of that year. The cartoon, a play on the 1928 Warner Bros. feature *The Singing Fool*, starring Al Jolson, also featured the first onscreen credits for Dietrich as the studio's musical director. It also represented the first onscreen credits for Tex Avery and Lester Kline as animators.

In further retooling the series, Walter made more welcome changes that year: giving Oswald a consistent speaking "voice." He pegged animator Pinto Colvig, who had voiced a hippo character in the July 1930 cartoon *Spooks*, to become the first to voice his cartoon rabbit. Colvig started with the August release, *Henpecked,* which Walter also single-handedly directed and for which he provided the voice of one of the rabbit's many nephews. Colvig again lent his voice to Oswald in the November 1930 release, *The Navy.*

With the early December release of the 22nd *Oswald* cartoon, *Africa,* which recycled animation from the color sequence in the 1930 Universal feature *King of Jazz,* Walter and Nolan introduced another refreshing component: the series' first theme song, "OSWALD (The Lucky Rabbit)." With music by James Dietrich and lyrics by Bernie Grossman, the new element went over well with moviegoers and critics. As a critic for the *Motion Picture Herald* noted in his review of the *Oswald* cartoon, *Mars,* which Walter and Nolan codirected and released in late December: "When Oswald and Peg Leg flirt with a girl in the park, Oswald receives a kick that perches him on Mars. Oswald sings the 'Lucky Rabbit' number, while some particularly unique and unusual effects are achieved in cartoon work. The theme song idea for the shorts is one of the most striking ideas yet introduced into animated cartoons."

As successful as his *Oswald the Lucky Rabbit* cartoon series had become, Walter had only scratched the surface of his potential in the sound age. Some of his best work was yet to come.

Knock-Knocking
His Way to the Top

By 1931, with the Great Depression threatening his future and that of his studio, Walter was forced to make cutbacks. To survive, he shortened the lengths of films to cut costs and produced only 18 new theatrical shorts that year. With James Dietrich, he added soundtracks to six originally silent Disney *Oswald* cartoons—*Trolley Troubles, Mechanical Cow, Oh Teacher, All Wet, Great Guns,* and *Ocean Hop*—reissuing them to theaters through April 1932.

In the late fall of 1931, Walter turned over the voice of Oswald to a nine-year-old child actor by the name of Mickey McGuire, whose real name was Joe Yule Jr. and who later became known to the world as Mickey Rooney. He had become a rising star in the popular two-reel Mickey McGuire live-action comedies, based on the *Toonerville Trolley* comics, for the R-C Pictures Corporation before signing to become the new voice of Oswald. The young star only voiced the character in two known cartoons, *The Hare Mail*, released in late November, and *The Fisherman*, issued in early December, which Walter and Nolan codirected. Walter once said of Mickey, "He was just a wild kid then. Because of his age, he had the right squealing voice for Oswald. We'd sit down to do some dialogue with him, then take a rest, and then we had to run all over the lot to find him because he was probably in the rafters or somewhere. Mickey was cute—he did a terrific job!"

Walter later replaced Rooney with female voice artist Bernice Hansen. She was perhaps best known as the squeaky-voiced Sniffles the Mouse of Warner Bros. cartoon fame, who sounded much like Oswald. She voiced Oswald for the duration of the series' run. "She had a very peculiar voice," Walter said in an interview. "She had a natural little baby voice. She was only 40 years old."

Meanwhile, by the summer of 1932, to further bolster his studio's coffers, Walter created and introduced a new character and secondary cartoon series, *Pooch the Pup*. These Bray-like comical adventures featured a little tramp with a bundle on his back walking down the railroad tracks with his pesky pup. Shouldering the responsibility of producing and directing two series at once would have been difficult at best, so Walter divided the studio into two separate units of animators. Walter directed *Pooch the Pup* and Nolan worked solely on *Oswald*. (This would become a source of consternation, however, as both were credited as codirectors on the *Oswald* series, including films Nolan alone directed and his unit animated without Lantz.) Walter was grateful to have Nolan as his codirector as he was a very competent helmsman and as budget-conscious as Walter. He never went over budget, and as Walter said, "He was always right on the mark."

That August, Walter's *Pooch the Pup* delighted moviegoers in his first entry, *The Athlete*, a spoof of the 1932 summer Olympics held in Los Angeles, California. Of the character's origin, Walter once told the author, "The situations were like this: there was a little tramp with a small bundle on his back walking down the railroad track with his dog, Pooch. The stories were like the ones I made for Bray—like Dinky Doodle. I got the idea from those, using similar situations." Some familiar stories that Lantz relied on were children's fairy tales. He found them to be most rewarding vehicles in terms of good stories and first-rate characterizations. Fairy tales had a cult following of their own and Lantz was just popularizing the art by producing them for the screen. Enhancing the beauty of each production was very stylish animation that added to the film's authenticity.

Hollywood trade advertisement touting Lantz's two starring characters, Oswald the Lucky Rabbit and Pooch the Pup, in 1932. *(Courtesy: Walter Lantz)*

Four additional *Pooch the Pup* cartoons that Walter directed rounded out the year, including *The Butcher Boy, The Crowd Snores* (a takeoff of the 1932 Warner Bros. feature *The Crowd Roars*), *The Under Dog,* and *Cats and Dogs.* In 1933, he directed five more Pooch cartoon comedies in the series, among them *Merry Dog, The Terrible Troubadour, Pin Feathers, Hot and Cold,* and *King Klunk,* a satire of the RKO Radio Pictures feature *King Kong.* Of these, his best is *Hot and Cold.* The cartoon is shaped around an old film tune, "Turn on the Heat," which was originally scored for the 1929 Fox feature *Sunny Side Up.* The story is rather clever, in that a weather king who lives at the North Pole tries controlling the climate. Pooch tries convincing the weather king to return the climate back to normal.

That same year, Walter and Doris moved into a stylish 7,000-square-foot home in nearby Toluca Lake. It was the first art deco house built in Los Angeles, a scaled-down replica of Danny Hall's art deco, post-Bauhaus sets in the Universal feature *Magnificent Obsession.*

With the *Pooch the Pup* series concluding in 1933, Walter returned to directing the *Oswald the Lucky Rabbit* series. He and Nolan still headed separate animation units, occasionally "switching off" beginning in mid-1934 in terms of who managed which unit. One of Walter's stellar efforts in 1933 was the November 27 release, *The Merry Old Soul.* The *Motion Picture Herald* called the short "an amusing and clever cartoon." The film was based on a familiar formula: using caricatures of famous film personalities. Walter found the idea so intriguing that he produced this series of similar cartoons. This charming first effort situates Oswald in a tooth-pulling episode with his dentist. After the dentist gives him the gas, Oswald dreams that Old King Cole, deep in the blues, needs some cheering. He manages to bring the king out of his doldrums with the aid of caricatured comedians and others representing Charlie Chaplin, Greta Garbo, Ed Wynn, Laurel and Hardy, Joe E. Brown, Will Rogers, W.C. Fields, Al Jolson, Mae West, Jimmy Durante, Harold Lloyd, Zasu Pitts, and the Marx Brothers. The cartoon marked yet another important achievement, becoming Walter's first cartoon to be nominated for an Academy Award, only to lose to Walt Disney's *Three Little Pigs.*

In 1934, Walter made it his main objective to beat out Disney, and consequently the *Oswald* cartoons he directed came across, in Walter's own words, as "too cutesy," with a few exceptions. One worthy effort is *The Toy Shoppe*. Released in early February, the film makes use of a Disney/Harman and Ising story where the toy shop comes to life after dark. It is one of the series' brightest ventures, with a remarkable combination of splashy backgrounds and character movements. Another honorable mention is *Kings Up*, which debuted on movie screens that March. The film is every bit as explosive as the dialogue sung in this light opera. Oswald, hoping to gain knighthood from the Queen, battles the villainous Black Knight. He puts away the dastardly knight and wins the Queen's hand in marriage in the end. It was not until that year—not since his cameo appearances in the first animated sequence in two-strip Technicolor in 1930's *King of Jazz*—that Walter would feature Oswald in his own color sound cartoons, *Toyland Premiere* and *Springtime Serenade*. After that, Walter returned to producing them in black-and-white, except for the last cartoon in the series.

That year, Walter made one noticeable and historic change to his team of artists, promoting La Verne Harding to animator on his *Oswald the Lucky Rabbit* series, starting with "Wolf! Wolf!" She became only the second woman in history to become a full-fledged animator at a major cartoon studio (the first was Fleischer animator Lillian Friedman), a position she held at Walter's studio until 1960. During later work on the *Woody Woodpecker* series, she would be responsible for designing the version of the character in use after 1950. As Walter later remembered, "La Verne came to me with a beautiful portfolio, so I gave her a job as an inbetweener. She became one of my top animators . . . Most producers didn't believe a woman could draw the exaggerations needed for action, that they could only handle birds and bees and flowers. They were wrong, of course."

Later that year Walter presented theater exhibitors with his third cartoon series, *Cartune Classics*, a series of two-strip color fairy tales trying to copy the success of Disney's three-strip Technicolor *Silly Symphonies* series. The films were basically musicals, with more music and sound effects than dialogue incorporated into the films. The first entry released in early October was a deluxe version and contemporary satire of the Brothers Grimm's popular fairy tale *The Elves and the Shoemaker*. Walter directed and produced the hugely successful cartoon, which was called *Jolly Little Elves*. Costarring Oswald the Lucky Rabbit and Pooch, the eight-minute short marked Walter's return to doing color for the first time, due to the expense, since producing the first two-color Technicolor sequence in the color feature *King of Jazz*.

The cartoon was so well received that in 1935, it was nominated for Walter's second Academy Award, but Disney's *Silly Symphony* cartoon, *The Tortoise and the Hare*, won the gold statuette. Walt Disney was reportedly worried about the competition Walter's *Cartune Classics* posed, but his concerns were short-lived as Universal was unwilling to finance Walter to produce all-color cartoon shorts. Thus, his color *Cartune Classics* came to an abrupt end after only two years. He directed only four more *Cartune Classics* fairy tale spectacles, including *Toyland Premiere* (1934), in which loads of Hollywood film stars join Oswald the Lucky Rabbit in the fun, including Bing Crosby, Laurel and Hardy, Shirley Temple, and others. The others, all created in 1935, were *Candyland* (1935), *Three Lazy Mice* (1935), and *Fox and the Rabbit* (1935).

That year, Walter's relationship with Nolan ran aground as a serious rift developed between them when Nolan was helming what turned out to be his "last hurrah," the patriotic classic, *Confidence*. In this cartoon, Walter's famed film rabbit seeks the help of President Franklin D. Roosevelt to solve a crisis with his chicken ranch left in a terrible state as a result of the Great Depression. Nolan's contract was up but reportedly Walter offered him a "lower wage" than he considered acceptable. Nolan refused the offer, so Walter replaced him with "less expensive directors." Subsequently Nolan left the studio in 1934, his final Oswald becoming *Spring in the Park*, before he found work at Charles Mintz and later Fleischer studios.

After Nolan's departure, Walter reorganized all the animators into a single unit, even though most did not stay much longer. After codirecting two known *Oswalds* (possibly *The Hillbilly* and *Towne Hall Follies*) with Lantz in 1935, Tex Avery also departed, with ex-Nolan animators Sid Sutherland, Virgil Ross, Joe D'Igalo, and Jack Carr following.

LAUNCHING HIS OWN STUDIO

Walter would have to wait to make more sweeping changes, however. Amid a corporate upheaval with Universal forcing Carl Laemmle Sr. and his son, Carl Jr., from power, one unpleasant management decision was to shut down the animation studio. To some, this would have spelled disaster; to Walter, it spelled a new opportunity. Going against the trend Universal itself had started, he won the right to turn the animation studio into a separate entity under his direct control, making him a mini-mogul of his own animation production company, still on the Universal lot. Thus, on November 16, 1935, Walter Lantz Productions was born.

Under the new contract, renewable thereafter on a yearly basis, Universal would handle distribution of his films, calling for him to produce a specific number of films each year—usually 26—with them advancing him an agreed-upon weekly cash amount that eventually rose from $2,583.33 to $3,750 to cover his production costs. Once costs were recouped, Walter received 25 percent of the profits, with Universal controlling rights to his cartoons. Shortly thereafter, Walter named Victor McLeod as his full-time story man, a position he held until 1940. He also instigated another major change, assigning animator Manuel Moreno to redesign Oswald because "Disney was also changing his characters."

Starting with 1935's *Case of the Lost Sheep*, released in early December 1935, the new-look Oswald appeared for the first time. He was drawn as a cuter, white-furred (instead of black), and more realistic rabbit. This was after animators had applied Moreno's new "model" two months earlier for a non-Oswald bunny in the two-strip Technicolor cartoon, *Fox and the Rabbit*, the last of Walter's *Cartune Classics*. Such changes, however, did not translate into greater success than the previous version in new and upcoming releases. Instead, Oswald was the least appealing in films that overall were not very entertaining, despite Walter's efforts in the next three years to "spruce things up." He added several new supporting characters, including Elmer the Great Dane, a frequent costar first seen in the self-titled *Oswald* cartoon that April; the cute litter of ducklings, Fee, Fi, Fo, Fum,

Lantz proudly shows off character drawings of his madcap simians, Meany, Miny, and Moe, who he directed in their own series of theatrical cartoon misadventures in the 1930s.

and Phooey, who first appeared in 1936's *The Barnyard Five* (1936); a bizarre rooster, Dumb Cluck (created by Charles Bowers), first starring in the 1937 *Oswald* short, *The Dumb Cluck*, and happy-go-lucky Snuffy Skunk (who looks more like a squirrel), first costarring in the 1938 *Oswald* cartoon, *Yokel Boy Makes Good*.

Among the most entertaining of the new characters was a trio of Stooge-esque monkeys, Meany, Miny, and Moe (originally called on model sheets, "Meany, Miny, and Mo"). Walter unleashed them on audiences in the November 1935 *Oswald* cartoon *Monkey Wretches*, which he directed. Feeling they had real potential, he featured them the following March in a second *Oswald* cartoon he helmed, *Beauty Shoppe*, and a third he directed in late May, *Farming Fools*. At the end of the year, he spun them off into their own successful series that he produced and directed—the fourth for Universal. These madcap circus-dressed sapiens acted entirely in pantomime, like great silent film comedians Charlie Chaplin and Harry Langdon (two of Walter's favorites), incorporating the kind of broad slapstick comedy gags that made the Columbia Pictures live-action comedy trio, the Three Stooges, so famous.

Between 1936 and 1937, Walter featured them in 13 cartoons, the first being *Turkey Dinner*. According to a story in *Variety*, he cut his commitment of *Oswald the Lucky Rabbit* cartoons in half to produce the 13 planned *Meany, Miny, and Moe* cartoons, budgeted at $8,250 each, $250 more than his *Oswald* cartoons with the added expense of animating three characters. He had many fond memories of series and characters, once recalling, "They were just three lively monkeys who got tangled in all sorts of situations. I recall one in particular where they were going to play golf. One was a caddy, one drove a cart, and the other was a kibitzer—and they just had one terrific time on the golf course. They had trouble with the cart, wrecked the golf course, and got in all sorts of trouble."

The cartoon Walter referred to is *The Golfers*, the first 1937 production and one of the series' best. A critic for *Motion Picture Herald* opined, "The finale of the monks' score with a robot golf machine provides some rapid fire and occasionally humorous situations. The youngsters, of course, and perhaps the golf minded of the audience will find something in the gags to chuckle about."

In their few appearances to date, the likeable characters gained, as a critic for *Box Office* magazine wrote, "a following among cartoon addicts." Another notable addition worthy of plaudits was *House of Magic* (1937), in which the trio of mischief makers take refuge in a house of magic, stocked with "multiplying rabbits, magic hats, and all the necessities," during a huge storm. In *The Big Race* (1937), the three chimps win a top prize in a big auto race after a "breathless" ride across the finish line in a heap to win the $5,000 purse from ace contender, Barney Hippo. In *The Steel Workers* (1937), called an "average program filler which will amuse cartoon fans," the three work as riveters on a construction site where they engage in the usual tomfoolery with "hot rivets, grappling hooks, and iron girders" with the entire steel framework tumbling to the ground in a rough-and-tumble finish.

Another well-reviewed film Walter directed in the series was the seventh overall, *The Stevedores*, released on May 24, 1937. A critic for *Box Office* magazine wrote: "The imaginations of the script man and animators ran rampant in making this cartoon, and the resultant comedy is hilarious." This time around, the three lazy monkeys are working for a bulldoggish captain on a freight vessel at sea. Moe ends up taking an unexpected dunk in the ocean after having trouble moving a piano while Meany becomes drunk on pickled herrings. By the finale, it is "if you can't beat 'em, join 'em," with the monkeys and the captain all pleasantly inebriated.

Walter often credited the use of pantomime as one major reason for the series' success. As he stated in an interview, "They were more like the Three Stooges, where the action was very physical gags and broad action. We didn't need any dialogue because they were doing the kind of pantomime like Charlie Chaplin and Harry Langdon. They didn't need to talk to be funny. Neither did these characters."

In late 1937, Walter discontinued production of the *Meany, Miny, and Moe* series after three out of their last four films that year—*Fireman's Picnic, Ostrich Feathers*, and *Rest Resort*—garnered mostly unfavorable reviews as "aimless and lacking in entertainment appeal," with the possibilities of his three cute characters not properly "utilized" for laughs with material that "doesn't make them funny," as some critics wrote. As Walter confessed, "There just wasn't much else we could do with the characters."

Earlier in his career, Walter had begun the practice—as did many other animators—of featuring popular celebrities in his cartoons.

In fact, he once created a concept for a new original theatrical short series called *Seeing Stars*. The films were to feature cartoon caricatures of famous Hollywood film personalities, something done in more outlandish fashion by his contemporaries at Warner Bros. in the late 1930s and 1940s. As he told Hollywood gossip columnist Hedda Hopper, stars "loved it," but once their agents started demanding 10 percent of the gate in exchange for using their likeness, he dropped the idea altogether.

When Walter exactly proposed the series remains a mystery, but he may have concocted the idea in 1937. That year, he proceeded to produce a new cartoon short to launch this potential series, called *Hollywood Bowl*. Directed by Elmer Perkins and animated by Frank Tipper and Merle Gilson, the cartoon featured animated caricatures of many famous show business notables, including Leopold Stokowski, Hugh Herbert, Greta Garbo, Groucho Marx, Bing Crosby, Charlie McCarthy, W.C. Fields, Clark Gable, Charles Laughton, Joe E. Brown, Katherine Hepburn, Fats Waller, Rudy Vallee, Martha Raye, Benny Goodman, Cab Calloway, Fred Astaire, and Jack Benny. In this mildly entertaining short, Stokowski's expressive hands were shown "getting stuck in a woman's hair curlers."

The world-famous conductor apparently did not find the joke funny and threatened to sue. Walter shelved the film. After Universal signed Stokowski to star in a major role opposite Deanna Durbin in a feature released in September 1937, *100 Men and a Girl*, he reportedly dropped his threat and reconsidered, with the cartoon subsequently being released in October 1938 as the last cartoon under the *New Universal Cartoon* banner.

After that experience, Walter principally focused on creating his own characters. Between 1938 and 1939, with his studio's signature star, Oswald the Lucky Rabbit, wearing thin on audiences, he began experimenting with new characters and ideas to put his studio on the map. He unveiled two new series of continuing and one-shot cartoons, the aforementioned *New Universal Cartoon* (in reference to the studio's post-Laemmle management) and *Comedy Cartunes*. The latter introduced the boyish Baby-Face Mouse, director Alex Lovy's knockoff

Stock 1938 movie poster for Walter Lantz *Cartune* shorts featuring his studio's stable of stars, including Andy Panda, Baby-Face Mouse, Fo, Fi, Fum, and Phooey, Elmer the Great Dane, Meany, Miny, Moe, Oswald the Lucky Rabbit, and others. *(Courtesy: Walter Lantz)* © *Walter Lantz Productions. All rights reserved.*

of Warner Bros. Sniffles the Mouse, who strays from home and comes face-to-face with a myriad of wise-guy rodents and rat gangsters (with the mantra: "Crime does not pay"). In 1938, he unveiled a third series, *Mello-Dramas*, lampoons of 1890s melodramas following the exploits of a damsel-in-distress, Nell, rescued by her handsome but thick-headed Swedish boyfriend, Dan, from a dastardly mustached villain. Then, a year later, he added *Li'l Eightball*, the adventures of an ingenious black boy created by director Burt Gillett, who worked briefly for Walter's studio, in his first of the Walter Lantz *Comedy Cartunes, A Haunting We Will Go*. It was also Walter's studio's first cartoon in three-strip Technicolor.

Walter added other potential characters to his studio's roster hoping they would become stars in their own right. In 1938, one such property he adapted was Gene Brynes's popular comic strip, *Reg'lar Fellers*. Walter made it into a black-and-white cartoon with hopes of it becoming a series, *Boy Meets Dog!* Made originally for Ipana Toothpaste and for theatrical release, the film was never distributed theatrically but released many years later to the home movie market by Castle Films. Other characters Walter brought to the screen included: Les Kline's "Simple Simeons," Jock and Jill, in three cartoon shorts starting with 1938's *Ghost Town Frolics*; Elmer Perkins' top-hatted cuckoo bird, Charlie Cuckoo, in 1939's *Charlie Cuckoo*; and famous illustrator Willy Pogany's cute flute-playing, mischief-making boy satyr, Peterkin (based on a story written by his wife called, "Peterkin Pan") in the first and only full Technicolor Peterkin cartoon, 1939's *Scrambled Eggs*.

Until 1939, Walter featured his once biggest star, Oswald the Lucky Rabbit, in new cartoons before ending production after 10 straight years. "We just ran out of ideas. We had done just about everything imaginable," he said. Walter directed four out of the five final shorts he produced, including *The Lamp Lighter, Man Hunt, Yokel Boy Makes Good*, and *Trade Mice*. This was not before tinkering some more with the drawing style of the character before he vanished from the screen, as evident in 1938's *Happy Scouts*, the second-to-the-last *Oswald* cartoon, in which the rabbit's fur is a combination of white and gray.

Five years later, however, Walter's famed rabbit made an encore in the 195th *Oswald* cartoon released as part of his studio's *Swing*

Symphonies series, *The Egg-Cracker Suite* (1943). Thereafter Oswald lived on as a popular star of Dell Comics's *New Funnies* comic books launched the previous year. Eight years later, Walter permanently retired him after making a final cameo appearance in the three-strip Technicolor *Woody Woodpecker* cartoon, *The Woody Woodpecker Polka*.

CREATING CARTOON PANDA-MONIUM

After pulling the plug on his *Oswald the Lucky Rabbit* series, and with none of his previous characters packing enough "star power" to catch on with audiences, it became evident to Walter that he needed a new cartoon to distinguish his studio from others. After a woman donated a giant panda to the Chicago Zoo, sparking national attention, an idea struck him: why not a cartoon panda?

Walter flew to Chicago to see the cub, Su-Lin, one of only two live pandas in the world on exhibit, up close and to take photos and draw sketches of her. His arrival in the Windy City coincided with that of a Universal newsreel cameraman, who captured footage of Su-Lin that became a useful point for reference for Walter and his animation crew. Months later, Walter introduced animation's first cartoon panda—one that took off immediately and was highly marketable and, more importantly, a character he owned: the lovable Andy Panda.

In late May 1939, Walter gave *Los Angeles Times* columnist Philip K. Scheuer, who penned the weekly studios and theater gossip column, a unique advance preview of his newest character. He introduced Andy to the famed scribe via a Movieola, a device used in editing rooms that runs the film under a magnifying glass and a light with the images projected onto a tiny screen. Walter stood over his shoulder, supplying the dialogue as the film cranked along. As Scheuer gushed, "Andy looked good to me—more baby than giant, a cross between a polar and brown bear, striped like a devil's food cake. He was in Technicolor and cute as the dickens."

That September, Walter featured his cuddly character for the first time in *Life Begins for Andy Panda*, directed by Alex Lovy, who was largely responsible for devising the character from Walter's sketches and from photos and newsreel footage. This premier short, costarring Snuffy Skunk and a slow-talking turtle, Mr. Whippletree, deals with the birth of Andy, how he grows up only to be captured by pygmy panda hunters after wandering off in the jungle against the advice of his father (Papa Panda), and how he is rescued. The film itself was a major hit and Walter moved forward with producing two more films, essentially following the same formula as before: *Andy Panda Goes Fishing* (1939), directed by Burt Gillett, and *100 Pygmies and Andy Panda* (1940), with Lovy again directing.

In 1937, the unexpected gigantic success of Walt Disney's first full-length color feature, *Snow White and the Seven Dwarfs*, prompted several other cartoon studios to announce plans to produce their own animated features, including Max Fleischer's planned adaptation of *Gulliver's Travels* and Paul Terry's animated feature-length treatment of *King Lear* with his Farmer Alfalfa in the titular role. Many of the films announced were never made. After criticizing the Rotoscoped look (a technique in which animators trace over live-action movements of actors, frame by frame) of the animation in Disney's *Snow White*, Walter sought to boost his studio's image by producing full-length animated features, declaring plans to produce *Aladdin and the Wonderful Lamp* (also titled as *Aladdin and His Lamp*) at a budget of $500,000. Unlike Disney's use of Rotoscope, Walter declared he would use the technique only for "timing" because of its inherent limitations as evidenced in *Snow White*. As he said at the time, "This literal system resulted in two faults—a jittering movement that contrasted with the fluidity of the animals, and the fact that the human characters were too accurate to be seen beside the caricatures."

Production of the feature, like many others Walter announced, never materialized. In late December 1939, he reportedly departed on a two-week trip to New York to "arrange for financing . . . and probably also a releasing deal" for three different feature properties he wanted to develop. Walter owned the rights to all three, his versions of popular children's stories: *Jack, the Giant Killer*; *The Old Woman Who Live in a Shoe*; and *Pandora's Box*, which, as *Los Angeles Times* columnist Edwin Schallert wrote, would likely create "controversy with the Fleischers over

'Pandora' because they have already named that theme as one of theirs [next films]."

Walter even later attempted to adapt *Ali Baba and the Forty Thieves,* a property owned by Universal. The comedy would have featured caricatures of Abbott and Costello, Universal's top comedy film stars at the time, and real burlesque comedians as the "thieves." Universal only committed to a $400,000 budget but Walter estimated he needed $1 million. Like all of his previous feature film plans, financing was an issue and the project proved "too costly and too much of a risk," he once said. "There were times when I would have liked to have produced a feature cartoon . . . We could have done the things Disney did but nobody had his money. Disney had his own studio while I was on a weekly salary; if we went over budget, I was sure to hear about it."

A few months into 1940, however, Walter faced a major crossroads in his career when Universal told him they would continue to distribute his cartoons but no longer finance them. As he later reflected, "I think everyone gets breaks in the luck. The trick is recognizing opportunity when it comes, then develop it."

This left Walter, whose studio had operated as an independent entity since 1935, scrambling for alternative sources for funds, mortgaging and hocking everything he could to raise the money to produce future cartoons at a cost of $9,000 per short. As he later told the author, "I needed $28,000. I borrowed on my house, my car, my furniture, everything I had, but I could only raise $14,000. So I went around to everyone I knew in Hollywood" to raise the difference.

In exchange, Walter offered potential suitors a half-interest for the additional $14,000 in funds. He thought his offering was a great investment opportunity and a bargain, especially since famed automaker Henry Ford started the Ford Motor Company with only $28,000. Remarkably, he found no takers. Those he approached either said they could not or would not invest.

On January 23, 1940, Universal advanced Walter's last weekly check, and a month later he was forced to close his studio without the necessary resources to continue. Only his accountant, Bob Miller, still drew a weekly paycheck. Meanwhile Walter won one concession from

Lantz's first major character of his creation, Andy Panda, as featured on the front cover of an issue of the popular Dell Comics series that ran from 1943 to 1962.

Universal: They surrendered to him all copyrights, trademarks, and film and merchandising rights to his characters in his cartoons from the previous four years, meaning he owned Oswald the Lucky Rabbit and Andy Panda outright.

Many of his extremely loyal staff members, however, returned to complete one cartoon and the fourth *Andy Panda* short that Walter produced and directed, *Crazy House*. Afterward, he used the film as leverage to sign a seven-year contract with Universal to exclusively distribute his films that included the studio cosigning with him on a $10,000 loan from the Irving Trust in New York, from which he paid the artists that had worked on the film. Thus, he became a power separate from Universal and something of a maverick in the animation industry. "I was the only producer, except Disney," he later stated, "who financed his own pictures, so I now own my films."

Because of his studio's closure during the year, Walter produced only eight cartoons for release that year, directing seven, including *Crazy House*, his first fully independent cartoon. In this first directing effort, Andy takes a pleasant drive with his Papa but gets stalled, and they have to stay the night at a "crazy house" where all sorts of strange and funny things occur. As a whole, a critic for *Showman's Trade Review* called it "a satisfactory Technicolor cartoon that won't make or break any program."

In his earliest adventures, Andy was simply a "cute little panda bear" who was not clothed. But as the series went along, Walter modified the character, giving him a little hat, a pair of pants, and shoes that "made him into a very cute character," he said. Later in the series, Andy's father, Papa Panda, was incorporated into the adventures, adding a whole new dimension to the stories, with Andy always correcting his pop because of various incidents where he would screw things up. "And Andy, of course, seemed to have more brains than his father," Walter added. "That was the format, more or less."

After different actors tried to do the character's voice—first Bernice Hansen from 1939 to 1940, and then Sara Berner from 1941 to 1944—Walter Tetley assumed the role until the character's final cartoon in 1949, doing, in Walter's opinion, "a very fine job."

BREAKING THE MOLD WITH A WOODPECKER

In 1940, after enjoying modest success with only one headline character, Walter still sought to create a breakthrough star that would distinguish his studio. In late October, he introduced a new albeit short-lived
character, Punchy, bearing a remarkable resemblance to Tex Avery's
bulbous-nosed bumpkin, Egghead, of Warner Bros. cartoon fame, in
the Technicolor *Cartune* short, *Recruiting Daze*. Then, a month later in
only the second *Andy Panda* cartoon he directed, *Knock Knock*, he finally
struck pay dirt with a lunatic bird featured in a secondary role opposite
his likeable panda and who produced gales of laughter on the screen:
Woody Woodpecker.

For many years, the stories Walter and studio publicists spun to
the press about Woody's origin were often aberrations of the truth.
In 1940, Walter and Doris, who had grown apart in their marriage,
divorced as did Grace Stafford and George Duryea. Subsequently, Walter and Grace rekindled their relationship and were married in a small
Methodist Church in Reno, Nevada. They honeymooned at a cabin
Walter owned in Lake Sherwood, a small, unincorporated resort community outside of Los Angeles, a mere 300 hundred yards from the
picturesque shoreline.

One story had it that Woody was the result of "a continuing nui-
sance" when Walter was busy at his drawing table while a woodpecker
outside was busy "drilling away" on a tree. The incessant noise got on
Walter's "nerves" until suddenly the idea of using the noisy woodpecker
as a cartoon character "flashed across his mind." The other story mixed
fact with fiction: While honeymooning, a raucous woodpecker caused
considerable damage to their cozy honeymoon cottage after which
Walter could not leave. Inspired by his wife's suggestion, "Make him
a cartoon character," they stayed, with Walter deciding to use the fine-
feathered intruder as an animated character.

In 1992, Walter told *The Los Angeles Times* a slightly different version: "We kept hearing this knock, knock, knock on the roof. And I said
to Gracie, 'What the hell is that?' So I went out and looked, and here's
this woodpecker drilling holes in the shingles. And we had asbestos
shingles, not wood. So, to show you how smart these woodpeckers are,

they'd peck a hole in the asbestos shingles and put in an acorn. A worm would develop in the acorn, and a week later the woodpecker would come back, get the acorn and fly away, letting out this noisy scream as he flew away." He added that Grace suggested doing the bird as a cartoon character, but admitted to her later he was "skeptical" of its potential.

In many other interviews, even with the author, Walter purported Woody's creation was inspired by the same real-life experience. That after marrying Grace, the newlyweds had scarcely begun their new lives together when a persistent little woodpecker pecked holes into the wooden roof of their cottage, resulting in some $200 in damages. As he explained, "We had this cottage in Lake Sherwood and there was this pesky woodpecker pecking on the roof every morning. My wife suggested that since I had animated animals like mice, rabbits and so forth, that maybe I should invent some kind of woodpecker character. I thought it was a good idea so I created Woody."

The stories, as intriguing as they sound, are a bit of a stretch as Walter and Grace were actually married on August 29, 1941, a whole year after Woody made his screen debut, after which Grace retired from show business. Whatever his inspiration, Woody became a largely appealing character to audiences and his appeal was simple: "He's a mischievous, likeable person who does things we'd like to but mustn't," Walter once said.

Not everyone was smitten with the idea, however, including East Coast film distributors who told him, "You must be out of your mind! This raucous bird will never go."

After his supposed honeymoon epiphany, Walter claimed he made a few drawings and took the idea into the studio where he talked it over with his animators and had Alex Lovy, one of his best artists, work on the design. Former Warner Bros. story man and director Ben Hardaway, who joined Walter's studio in 1940, developed a story for the first cartoon. To the contrary, some animators have claimed Hardaway, a man with a love for "screwball characters" in fact came up with Woody's original design. Hardaway had created the embryonic version of Warner Bros. "wild and wascally" rabbit, Bugs Bunny, in cartoons like *Porky's*

A 1941 model sheet of Lantz's machine-gun laughing, manic bird, whose original design he called "really ugly," the one and only Woody Woodpecker. *(Courtesy: Walter Lantz)* © *Walter Lantz Productions. All rights reserved.*

Hare Hunt and *Hare-Um Scare-Um,* and written the story for one of the early Daffy Duck cartoons, *Daffy and Egghead* (1938). In many respects, Hardaway's characterization possessed a high level of zaniness and vitality, unlike anything seen in cartoons Walter had produced since the early 1930s. In earlier films, even Woody's laugh sounds more like Hardaway's rabbit characters from his days at Warner Bros., voiced by none other than Mel Blanc.

Blanc, the first to voice Woody, recalled Hardaway proudly holding up a prototype drawing of Woody and asking him, "What do you think?"

Blanc, never one to mince words, replied, "Ugliest damn thing I ever saw."

As he wrote in his autobiography, *That's Not All, Folks!,* "And I was being polite. The original Woody was repulsive with a capital R. He had a peaked head topped with a sharply angled comb that looked like it had been styled in a wind tunnel. A narrow beak so long, its pointy tip was a zip code away. Short swollen arms and legs. In all, a sorry spectacle."

Truthfully, Woody was rather gruesome with a long bill, top knot, skinny yellow legs, and an all-blue body and, at first blush, not very appealing to the eye in his original form. Walter had a hard time explaining why Woody was designed the way he was other than to say, "I guess we considered woodpeckers as being really wild destructive creatures (which they aren't if you get right down to it)."

It was not the first or last time distributors would be out of step with the public. On November 25, 1940, *Knock Knock* opened in theaters, inducing a flurry of laughter from moviegoers and critics alike, who gave it generally high marks. It became another solid addition to Walter's *Andy Panda* series. Even *Showman's Trade Review,* not always known for giving Walter Lantz cartoons favorable marks, stated the film "is nevertheless better than the previous releases in this series and one that should entertain patrons, especially the kiddies."

Walter was rightfully upbeat about the character's success as preview crowds roared with laughter as Woody stole the picture, immediately launching him into stardom. "Woody was a hit the first time on the screen," he once said. As one scribe later wrote of Woody's mercurial success, "It wasn't long before the ubiquitous Woody laughed Andy clear off the screen."

Knock Knock is a truly fine cartoon that involves a marvelous conflict between brain and bird. The story opens with Andy asking Papa Panda if it's true that a bird can be caught by putting salt on its tail. Just before Papa can answer, he hears a knock-knock-knocking sound. That continuous pounding sound is none other than Woody Woodpecker pecking away at the cottage roof. Eventually the bird bores a hole through the roof and reaches down to tweak Papa's nose. Then, with a wide grin, Woody says, "Guess who?" before issuing his first "ha-hah-ah-ha-ha" laugh on the screen.

That prompts a wild chase as Papa grabs a rifle, wanting to rid the world of this menacing bird. Andy tags along with a salt shaker, hoping to prove that the legendary salt myth does work. As the chase winds down—with neither Papa nor Andy appearing they will be successful in catching Woody—Andy catches the raucous bird off guard and pours the entire shaker of salt on the bird's tail. Helplessly defeated, Woody cannot move but suddenly cries for help. Out of nowhere appear two other woodpeckers, one of whom tells Papa Panda, "Confidentially, this guy's crazy." Moments later, the other two woodpeckers join in on the chorus of "ha-hah-ah-ha-ha" laughs before hopping all over the place à la Daffy Duck's wild and exuberant exit hopping and yelling, "Woo-hoo! Woo-hoo! Woo-hoo! Woo-hoo! Woo-hoo!" in his second Warner Bros. cartoon, *Daffy Duck and Egghead* (1938).

Over the years, historians would draw parallels between Walter's Woody and Warner Bros. Daffy Duck, but Walter never bought into such theories, noting, "I don't even compare the two because Woody's personality is entirely different from Daffy's. Woody never really bothered anyone until he was taken advantage of. Then he really went to work on that person. Woody was a little wild at the beginning and he was really raucous and loud in all his actions. But he was never as wild as Daffy Duck."

As for Woody's incredible laugh, Walter turned to Blanc, best known as the voice of Warner Bros. characters Bugs Bunny, Daffy Duck,

Porky Pig, and many others. As Walter explained in an interview, "When we recorded the show, I asked Mel Blanc, who was to do Woody's voice, to think up some kind of laugh for more character. Mel tried a few versions and then came up with his distinguished contribution."

Blanc often credited Hardaway for suggesting the laugh and supposedly telling Walter, "We should give him a distinctive laugh and I know just who can do it: Mel Blanc."

Hardaway then called Blanc, who drove over to the studio to meet Walter to discuss doing the character.

Woody's crazy giggle—the first voice Blanc ever coined originally when he was a teenager—was nothing like the real thing but audiences did not seem to mind. Regarding the laugh-heard-'round-the-world that created so much onscreen merriment, Walter said, "It's [the laugh] not so farfetched. Listen sometime to the sound a real woodpecker makes as it flies away. It's a short, croaking sound. All we did was syncopate it and speed it up" by up to 15 percent in the films.

After finding Woody's physical features "really ugly" in his first cartoon, Walter changed his appearance as he would do other times over the course of Woody's career. As he stated, "We weren't totally satisfied with Woody. He was one of the most grotesque looking characters I had ever seen . . . But over the years, we modified him. That happens with a cartoon character. You look at the first Bugs Bunny, Mickey Mouse, or Donald Duck, and they didn't look anything like they do today. They've all gone through some changes, which is something you couldn't do with a live character."

Meanwhile Walter continued his efforts undeterred to establish his mark independently of Disney and Fleischer. On November 17, 1940, eight days before the debut of the first Woody Woodpecker cartoon, he unveiled to the press his latest venture—an amazing new plastic substance that permitted "smooth movement of inanimate figures." He had codeveloped it with independent film producer Edward Nassour for a series of stop-motion shorts he planned to produce called *Humanettes*. The substance, a unique blend of rubber and other materials, made "visible muscular movement as well as the smooth progress of the figures on the screen."

Walter believed in the process and went so far as to build a six-foot-square set in his studio, where he molded models of several prehistoric figures, supposedly shooting test footage of them. The new material was "notable for its smoothness. Because of the texture of the plastic and a new registering device, which guides and regulates the movement," wrote *New York Times* Hollywood correspondent Douglas W. Churchill, breaking the story that November, and saying, "He has secured a satisfactory illusion of lifelike action."

Walter and Nassour supposedly were on the heels of inking a deal with Columbia Pictures to use their new process in its epic feature *The Lost Atlantis.* As Churchill wrote, "While 'The Lost World,' made in 1925, has been regarded as a high point in screen magic, the method used to animate the animals in that film would not be successful today because the animation would seem amateurish in comparison with advances since made in other phases of production. The Lantz-Nassour development makes possible equaling the polish of the real-life portions of the picture, the inventors claim."

Walter reportedly filmed test footage of the process in both color and black and white. Although under exclusive contract with Universal for distribution of his cartoon shorts, he planned to make the process available for "the freelance market" while withholding it for feature films. At the time, his current plans were to use the test footage in one of his upcoming cartoon shorts to "find out what the public thinks about it."

In 1941, Walter produced a full slate of 13 theatrical cartoon shorts. Of these, he directed several other *Woody Woodpecker* cartoons, including *Woody Woodpecker* (1941), the first cartoon in the series to use the character's name in the title and the first featuring Blanc as the character's voice. The film also featured for the first time Woody's own theme song ("Everybody thinks I'm crazy! Yes sirree, that's me, that's me . . .") and the famous "Ha-hah-ah-ha-ha" music in the opening. Originally titled, *The Cracked Nut,* the film opens with Woody under observation by his fellow forest animals, all half-disgusted by and half-terrified of the insane bird. They find the bird's loony behavior too much to bear, so they intimidate him into seeing a fox psychiatrist who is just as

Lantz displays a more pleasing to the eye rendering of his famous woodpecker, Woody. *(Courtesy: Walter Lantz)* © *Walter Lantz Productions. All rights reserved.*

insane as Woody. Woody's visit does not result in his being committed, but his doctor winds up in an asylum instead, acting crazed and jumping around, unable to put up with Woody's brash antics.

Walter helmed two more fine efforts that year starring his wild and woolly woodpecker. The first was *The Screwdriver* (1941). Rated as a generally "funny" cartoon by a critic for *Box Office*, Woody, the "wackiest character in recent months," makes life miserable for a motorcycle traffic cop as a "jerk" in his speed-happy jalopy, turning the courteous cop into a careless driver himself and a crazed lunatic who ends up in jail. The second was the clever and amusing Technicolor cartoon, *What's Cookin'?* (1941), bound to "bring chuckles from most patrons," wrote a critic for *Showman's Trade Review*. Ignoring the weatherman's warning to go south before winter, this time Woody battles a hunger-starved cat who stops at his home to escape a terrible blizzard outside and has visions of Woody as a "savory roast."

Blanc supplied the voice for Woody in the first four or five cartoons. After signing an exclusive contract to voice cartoons for Warner Bros., he was prohibited from portraying "the little redheaded troublemaker." Kent Rogers provided the voice of Woody for the first time in 1942 with the release of *Ace in the Hole* and others, including *The Loan Stranger* (1942) and *Ration Bored* (1942). In 1944, besides acting as a story man, Hardaway doubled as the new voice of Woody, first voicing the character in April's *The Barber of Seville*, produced by Walter and directed by James Culhane, and for the next five years through March 1949's *Drooler's Delight*.

Walter continued using Blanc's prerecorded laugh, even after he stopped playing Walter's most popular cartoon star, for most of the *Woody Woodpecker* cartoons that followed, including the 1948 novelty tune, "The Woody Woodpecker Song," for which the famous voice man said he did not receive "a single penny." Though he considered Walter a friend, he considered such use of voices as "enormously unfair" and subsequently sued the cartoon maker ("as a matter of principle," Blanc said) for more than one-half million dollars. The judge ruled against him, noting he failed to copyright his contribution. Even then, Walter settled with Blanc out of court.

5

Returning to the Helm

While Woody Woodpecker became a much-needed breakout star for his studio, Walter continued during the next two years to produce and direct *Woody Woodpecker* and *Andy Panda* cartoons along with a handful of *Cartune* specialties. These were largely well received, including Walter's third Oscar-nominated cartoon short, *Boogie Woogie Bugle Boy of Company "B."*

During this time, his *Andy Panda* series remained successful and popular with audiences, with Andy's father assuming a more humorous role and adding to the overall zaniness in films like *Mouse Trappers* and *Dizzy Kitty*. In 1941, Andy appeared solo for the first time in *Andy Panda's Pop*, with his father making his final appearance in 1942's *Under the Spreading Blacksmith Shop*. Andy was featured by himself as a headliner in his films starting with *Good-Bye Mr. Moth* (marking the debut of Sara Berner, previously the voice of Andy's mother, as the voice of Andy). It was not until Walter produced the ninth cartoon in the series, *Nutty Pine Cabin*, that Andy would appear as a grown adult.

As the popular panda came of age during World War II, Walter also featured him solo in a series of popular 1942–1943 war-themed and patriotic cartoons, among them, *Victory Garden*, *Air Raid Warden*, and *Canine Commandos*. He also introduced a new character—a drawling,

Lantz laughs while reading the latest issue of Walter Lantz *New Funnies* series of comic books first published in 1942 by Dell Comics featuring his characters in comic-book adventures.

country pigeon who shows a squadron of pigeons his muster and becomes a minor star, Homer Pigeon—in the comical wartime romp, *Pigeon Patrol.*

In December of 1941, Walter created, produced, and directed the first two releases—*$21 a Day (Once a Month)* and *The Hams That Couldn't Be Cured* (1942)—of a brand-new theatrical cartoon series based on popular jazz tunes of the day, *Swing Symphonies*. The ambitious all-Technicolor musical oddities, costing $9,500 to $12,000 per film to produce, were born out of Walter's love of musicals. He made 14 musical shorts through 1944, with one he produced, *Juke Box Jamboree* (1942), receiving his studio's fourth Oscar nomination. Future entries were directed by staffers Alex Lovy, Ben Hardaway, Emery Hawkins, James Culhane, and Dick Lundy. Walter hired the latter two to fill his place after calling it quits as a director in 1942.

Acting primarily as a producer, Walter ran the studio while developing new properties and ideas for the screen that garnered two more Oscar nominations. Woody Woodpecker's *The Dizzy Acrobat* (1943) and Andy Panda's *Fish Fry* (1944) brought the total of Academy Award nods to six in his studio's history. In early June 1943, Universal prepared 26 all-new Technicolor *Cartunes* produced by Walter for shipment to the European market after it reopened following the United States military's defeat of Germany in World War II.

Around this time, Walter announced plans for production of two *Cartunes* of his most famous characters, Woody Woodpecker and Andy Panda, featuring movable clay figures—or Humanettes—his famed stop-motion process that he and Nassour had developed in 1940. As the *Motion Picture Herald*, a Hollywood trade magazine, first reported in its June 2, 1943, edition: "The Humanettes, which are made of clay and measure six inches in height, are said to make it possible to give something resembling human expression to the characters."

As he did before in announcing his newfound process in 1940, Walter teased the press with news that he had produced and completed experimental footage in Technicolor of his Humanettes that he planned to schedule and show to the media in the future. Whether or not he would produce more or an entire series of Humanettes subjects would depend on exhibitor and public reaction to the two announced Humanettes *Cartunes* shorts.

In many respects, Walter's ambitious plan was to follow another already popular stop-motion series, George Pal's Oscar-winning *Puppetoons*, for Paramount Pictures. This time around, he seemed more determined than ever to see his plans come to fruition. In December 1944, he formed a separate company with Nassour, called Lantz-Nassour

Woody Woodpecker in an animated segment of George Pal's 1950 science-fiction feature, *Destination Moon*.

Humanettes, Inc., and even leased studio space in a building on Sunset Boulevard not far from the old Warner Bros. lot. He ultimately built a 60-by-75-foot sound stage for production of four *Humanettes* cartoons in color and combining live action with stop-motion animation. In the May 26, 1945, edition of *Box Office*, Walter revealed he and Nassour had "made some animated" *Humanettes* pictures together but shortly thereafter parted company. Walter carried on, intending to launch his own studio, Consolidated Pictures, to produce the *Humanettes* series on his own.

Unfortunately, despite this fascinating technique, Walter again abandoned the projects due to lack of financing and interest. As of this date, no records of any films or test footage have been uncovered, much less documentation supporting Lantz's original announcement of filing U.S. patents protecting his newfound technology.

SWINGING TO A NEW BEAT

Continuing in his capacity as a producer right up into the 1950s, Walter took some new directions along the way. In 1946, he put music to animation entirely different from his previous musical *Swing Symphony* cartoons. He employed a 50-piece orchestra loaned out to him at Universal to perform the acoustical classical music as the backdrop to his latest series *Musical Miniatures*. Budgeted at $30,000 apiece, Walter produced four lively renditions—and his studio's most expensive pictures ever made—including his eighth and ninth Oscar-nominated entries, his first, *The Poet & Peasant* (1946) and *Musical Moments from Chopin* (1947), both costarring Woody Woodpecker and Andy Panda—through 1948.

That same year he extended the resources of his small animation studio to produce and animate a brief cartoon segment for Republic Pictures's latest live-action Gene Autry feature, *Sioux City Sue*, released in late November. The footage was that of a purported *Ding-Dong Donkey* cartoon—a Paragon Pictures presentation of "A Lang Fantasy" about the budding romance between Ding-Dong and a long-lashed, umbrella-clad Jenny—that flickers to life on a movie theater screen as a theater audience looks on in the context of the film itself.

As Woody Woodpecker continued to rocket to fame, Walter's studio rode on his coattails. Certainly, this was the case in 1948, after releasing an original recording by Kay Kyser and his Orchestra, with vocals by Gloria Wood and Harry Babbitt, of "The Woody Woodpecker Song." At a time when Decca Records's top teen crooner Dick Haymes and Capitol Records singing sensation Peggy Lee were blazing the charts with their latest releases, the Columbia Records recording instantly skyrocketed, catching on with audiences that included teenagers. As Russ Naughton wrote in his May 23, 1948, "Record Ramblings" column for *The Hartford Courant* newspaper: "Here's a novelty tune that's as crazy as they come. The tune is based on the five note laugh of the screwy, red-headed Woodpecker of movie cartoon fame. The Kyser crew treats this amusing ditty in a sort of playful manner and with an easy, bounce tempo. Gloria Wood sings the lyrics on 'Woodpecker,' while the usually dignified Harry Babbitt takes the part of 'Woody.'"

Within 10 days after its release, the song became a huge hit, immediately selling more than 250,000 copies and more than one million copies that year. With Babbitt's cackling vocals, it hit number two on the singles charts and topped the hit parade for 13 consecutive weeks. As a result, Walter rushed into production a new Woody Woodpecker cartoon featuring the song. Released that August, *Wet Blanket Policy*, with only Babbitt's vocals heard in the cartoon, became the only cartoon short ever to receive an Academy Award nomination for "Best Song."

The year before, Walter attempted to renegotiate his deal with Universal's vice president, Matty Fox, but Fox demanded commercial and licensing rights to Walter's characters. Walter refused and instead inked a new distribution deal with George Bagnall of United Artists (UA), producing 12 cartoons for them before shutting down his studio again in 1949. This happened after UA shorted him on the percentages of the box-office receipts they were supposed to pay covering the production costs of his cartoons. With his loan with Bank of America topping out at over $250,000, the bank recommended he temporarily close his studio until the loan could be reduced. During his studio's hiatus, Universal complied with his request to reissue some of his older cartoons, generating revenue to help pay down his debt before he later reopened his studio in 1950. That year, his studio produced only a brief animated sequence featuring Woody Woodpecker for the George Pal feature film *Destination Moon*, released by Eagle-Lion Films in late June. Afterward, Walter came to terms with Universal on a new deal, producing seven new cartoons for release in 1951, all starring Woody Woodpecker (including two, *Puny Express* and *Sleep Happy*, originally storyboarded by Ben Hardaway and Heck Allen during the studio's time with United Artists).

GIVING WOODY A NEW VOICE

The Woody cartoon in Pal's science-fiction film *Destination Meatball*, a play on the movie's title, is significant as it marked the first time Walter's wife, Grace Stafford, provided the voice of Woody. In preparing to do the film and a new series of *Woody Woodpecker* cartoons for United Artists, Walter sought to replace Ben Hardaway as the voice of his world-famous woodpecker. Many candidates anxiously auditioned in hopes of being picked. After her husband originally turned her down because Woody was a boy, Grace taped her own audition and secretly added it to the other recordings. Much to his surprise, Walter picked his wife after hearing only the playback of each audition. As Grace once recalled, "I was no exception. The producer was on the spot. He could take no chances in making the right decision. Woody was too important a star to gamble."

The tapes for each candidate were numbered with the applicants' names only known by the sound man who sat in during the audition. After listening to some 50 taped auditions, Walter was completely satisfied with his wife's, unaware it was hers. He chose Grace because "she had very good diction" and he wanted someone who could read Woody's lines with a "throaty delivery" and simply picked the voice that matched the character the best. As Walter later remembered, "When we had the listening session, I didn't want to see the actors who were doing the voices. So they ran some recordings and I picked one—No. 7, I remember—and I said, 'Who's that?' And it was Gracie. She sneaked it in on me. I thought, 'Oh, God, no! What are people going to think if they find out the producer's wife is doing Woody's voice?'"

Basing her Woody laugh on a "bugle call," Grace brought new life to Woody and made him seem chirpier than in earlier cartoons. Even then, Walter was not sure how people would react, knowing that the voice of Woody was done by a woman, much less his wife. Walter first employed his wife in the 1951 *Woody Woodpecker* cartoon, *Puny Express,* providing Woody's "laugh" in all 1951–1952 releases, doing extensive dialogue for the first time in 1952's *Stage Hoax,* before she voiced the character regularly in 1953. It was by Grace's request that she did not receive any onscreen voice credit in Woody cartoons until receiving it for the first time in January 1958's *Misguided Missile.* Grace chose not to

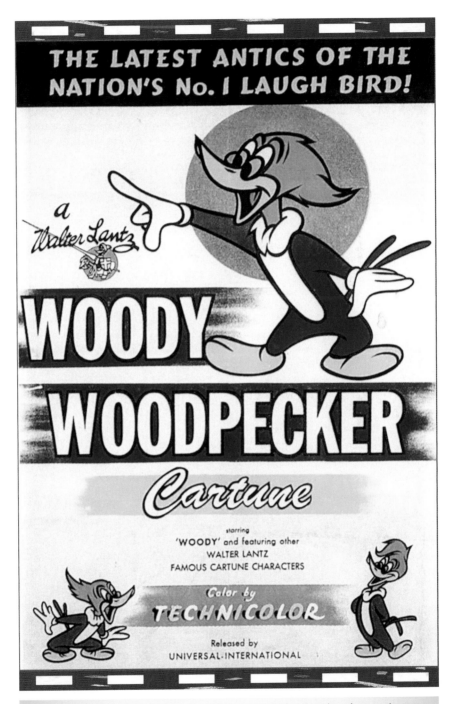

An original theatrical poster for Walter's Woody Woodpecker cartoons, circa 1950.

have her name listed because she did not want children to become disillusioned if they knew a woman had voiced Woody. As she explained in 1959, nine years after first doing the voice, "We thought at first children might not believe in Woody as much if they knew a woman provided

Lantz's feisty woodpecker became his top-selling licensed character in comic books and merchandise, including a series of "Tell a Tale" books for Whitman, among them, 1951's *Peck of Trouble*.

his voice. We know now we were wrong. At parties and visits to homes and friends I am frequently asked to 'laugh like Woody.' And youngsters love it."

In 1951, Walter returned to directing. His first cartoon coming back as a director was *Wicket Wacky*, which has Woody playing croquet and disturbing a gopher (identified on model sheets as "Goofy Gopher" but called "J. Goofer Gopher" onscreen) who is sleeping in his home underneath the croquet lawn. Woody ignores the gopher's pleas to stop as they fight to the finish, knocking each other out, only to emerge as friends in the end.

In all, Walter directed a total of seven cartoons that year—all of them starring Woody Woodpecker—including three exceptional efforts. In *Sling Shot 6 7/8*, Woody enters a shooting contest in a Western town and wins first prize with a slingshot as his weapon. A critic for *Box Office* crowed, "The Woodpecker's trick shots should get laughs." In *Redwood Sap*, Woody forgets to save food for the winter and his begging induces no sympathy from the forest denizens. *Woody Woodpecker Polka*, another lively effort, has Woody crash a barn dance for free eats. Wally Walrus becomes his escort and the two stage a slapstick struggle over food.

In 1952, Walter directed only four cartoons (all uncredited): *Born to Peck*, a film of flashbacks of Woody remembering the past when he was young, destructive, and sharp as a buzzard; *Stage Hoax*, in which Woody poses as a woman and hitches a stagecoach ride across the desert; *Woodpecker in the Rough*, featuring Woody as a golf maniac, and *Scalp Treatment*, costarring the adversarial Buzz Buzzard who tries scalping Woody as a gift to an Indian maden. Don Patterson directed two others. After this, Walter decided to hang it up as a director again.

Strictly working as a producer, Walter left it up to his staff of directors to churn out new animated shorts each year, promoting animator Paul J. Smith and subsequently Grant Simmons to the helm. He did not have much to worry about since his studio was running strong and his cartoons were still pulling in hefty box-office revenues. Woody was among the top-10 moneymakers in the short subjects field, an honor he upheld for about a decade. But Walter was not through. He had retired Andy Panda in 1949, leaving Woody as his studio's only major star, but in 1953, besides producing a short-lived series of comical *Foolish Fables,* he introduced a brand-new character created by Paul J. Smith. This Chaplinesque penguin, who scooted around street corners using Chaplin's trademark one-legged stand, was the contagiously funny Chilly Willy, a character that soon became as popular as Woody Woodpecker. The first cartoon, released on December 21, 1953, was *Chilly Willy.* Smith, whom Walter described as "a competent director and fantastic animator," also directed the pilot entry. Animating Chilly—a character that did all his actions in pantomime—was very difficult. Creating him and the action that appeared on the screen took "an awful lot of drawings and experienced animators," Walter once said.

Although Chilly was not an immediate success, following Tex Avery's return to working with Walter in 1954, as a director, Walter assigned him the task of resurrecting the "little fuzzy wuzzy" penguin, whom Avery did not find particularly funny and instead paired with much funnier costars. The first was *I'm Cold,* introducing Chilly's long-time costar, Smedley the dog, followed by *The Legend of Rockabye Point* (1955), Avery's last *Chilly Willy* and second to last film for Walter—nominated for his studio's ninth and tenth Academy Awards—vaulting Chilly to stardom.

By 1954, Walter was in a good place financially. Unlike Walt Disney, who took years to dig himself out of debt, he was completely debt free after once hocking everything he owned and borrowing the rest. Now he was worth a fortune. Despite taking as long as four years to recoup the cost for each cartoon, not including the cost of buying and equipping his studio, Walter continued producing with his gifted team of writers and directors—all of whom were cartoonists themselves—and artists and animators. They produced a total of 13 cartoons a year at a cost of $35,000 each. Walter was convinced that laughter was universal and did more for the human race than "all of the politicians." In his travels later that year to England, Spain, France, and Italy, he saw all the proof he needed that "humor is a common bond" as his cartoons garnered big laughs in theaters in which they played.

Walter's greatest competition that year came not so much from his peers and fellow animators but from a different industry altogether:

Lantz with his wife Grace, who took over as the voice of Woody in 1950.
(Courtesy: Walter Lantz)

comic books. With horror comics in particular becoming all the rage, he found it ironic to be going head-to-head with comics that in his opinion weren't "comics" in the true sense since the characters and stories were meant to frighten and "weren't funny." He thought they did not belong on newsstands with comics of popular animated characters. Besides the lamentable reading matter, he also had issue with most of the advertising in comic books, including ads for furniture, upholstery, auto parts, and weight-reducing gadgets exclusively aimed at adults. "What youngster," Walter asked in an interview, "could be interested in hormones and body-building exercises? Yet this is what you find in comic book ads."

In November of that year, Walter celebrated his 25th anniversary with Universal Pictures International. His cartoon comrade, Walt Disney, already a recipient of 22 Oscars and who was honored that same month with the prized Sylvania Award for his outstanding work on his *Disneyland* television series, actually headed the committee organizing the festivities for the anniversary celebration. Though his previous actions early in his career showed otherwise, Walter revealed at the time that neither of them looked upon each as a "competitor" and that any good cartoon they produced that entertained was good for each other's business.

As sensual screen stars like Ava Gardner, Marilyn Monroe, and Jane Russell steamed up movie screens in the 1950s, their highly charged performances were not the only ones to run afoul with Hollywood movie censors. Walter endured his own headaches trying to placate Production Code officials. In the fall of 1955, after decorated World War II hero-turned-actor Audie Murphy starred as himself in the critically acclaimed live-action feature, *To Hell and Back*, based on his autobiography of the same name, Walter decided to do a take-off of Murphy's film starring Woody Woodpecker, called *To Heck and Back*. Hollywood's censorship board took issue with the idea—nixing the word "heck."

It would not be the last time one of his creations came under fire. In earlier efforts, his famous woodpecker, Woody, was not allowed to milk a cow unless bossie wore "a skirt," or to kiss a girl (only the girls could kiss him), or utter something so nonoffensive as "gosh"; instead "golly" was deemed more appropriate. As Walter told famed gossip columnist Hedda Hopper in November 1954, "When you understand the reason for censorship stricter than any held over glamour girls, you relax. Though adults love them, cartoons are for kids and we've got to bend over backwards."

6

Taking His Act
to Television

By 1957, in his 28th year as a producer, Walter had produced by his estimation 600 cartoons for release through Universal Pictures with 13 additional shorts slated for production the following year. However, the future of the cartoon industry seemed particularly dim. In 1941, the cost to produce a single seven-minute, full-color theatrical cartoon was $15,000; 16 years later, producing the same high-quality cartoon in full animation had climbed to $75,000. By comparison, in the same period, the salaries he paid animators had soared from $70 to $225 a week, adding to his spiraling costs. At its zenith in 1947, 175 cartoon shorts were released to theaters that year; 10 years later, the number had dwindled down to 75, almost half of the total annual output.

While his cartoons were now more minimally animated, they were a minute or two shorter than those he made during Hollywood's golden age and cost an average of $35,000 to produce, not to mention another $10,000 for printing and distribution. Both skyrocketing costs and exhibitors paying only 15 percent more in booking fees than in prewar years meant the era of theatrical cartoon shorts was nearing an end. "Exhibitors still won't pay 25 cents extra for a booking," Walter explained at the time. "We're lucky to get $100 a week for a cartoon at a first-run theater. But the fee goes as low as $4 a week at second-run small-town [movie] houses."

The only survivors outside of Walter producing theatrical cartoon shorts were Walt Disney, Warner Bros., Terrytoons, and Paramount, with MGM closing its animation department that same year. It was taking him about four years to recoup his costs for each cartoon he produced, with revenue trickling in "driblets," as Walter complained, "If only the distributors would give us a tiny bit more, we might have a chance."

In October of that year, Walter warned that within five years, given its current course, production of animated cartoon shorts would cease altogether. "There'll always be a market for cartoons," he stated. "Even if no more cartoons are made, old ones will continue to be screened on a periodic basis."

In spite of his gloomy outlook, Walter reported he expected business for his studio—with an estimated value that year of $6 million—to increase. After 41 years in the cartoon business, he considered trading his drawing board for a fishing pole and retiring, but instead he would have the last laugh. As a result of the overall downward trend toward theatrical cartoon shorts, he expanded his enterprise to the small screen of television. In 1957, Walter developed his first half-hour television series, repackaging older cartoons originally shown in movie theaters, called *The Woody Woodpecker Show*. It came three years after the debut of Walt Disney's popular nighttime anthology series, *Disneyland*, on the same network, ABC. In announcing the program to the press, Walter said, "I'm aiming for the biggest teenage and adult audience of any cartoon show on TV."

The series came about when the cereal company Kellogg's was actively looking for a television cartoon series to sponsor and Woody seemed like the "logical bet." One caveat of the deal, however, was they also wanted Woody's creator, Walter, to appear in the series.

"I'm no actor," he said when the sponsors approached him with the idea.

After pondering the idea further, Walter relented under one condition: He would be able to tell kid viewers how animated cartoons were made. Kellogg's signed off on the idea, striking a deal with Leonard

Goldenson and the heads of ABC and commissioning 52 half-hours that season. Walter immediately went to work. Fortunately, he had a distinct advantage in producing the series: He had a huge backlog of cartoon shorts originally released to theaters from which to cull such a series.

One of the inherent difficulties Walter encountered in bringing the old films to the small screen was the overt racial stereotypes, sexual innuendo, and questionable acts that were considered violent or offensive by modern standards. As Wally Ruggles, production manager for the Leo Burnett Company, Kellogg's ad agency, stated at the time, "Kellogg doesn't want to make any enemies."

Unlike vintage *Tom and Jerry*, *Bugs Bunny*, and *Popeye* cartoons that used many of the same techniques he did, Walter never considered any cartoon he produced too violent. "I thought of them as slapstick comedies," he once said. "Nobody really bleeds or dies in these cartoons. If someone is shot full of holes, he is back to normal in the next scene; if his teeth fall out, he has a full set an instant later."

Kellogg's Cereal censors carefully scrutinized each cartoon, cutting or paring down 25 separate sequences, excluding any black stereotype caricatures, drinking scenes, and other material deemed too risqué for inclusion in the series' original 26 half-hours. Examples of scenes expunged or edited were a drunken horse setting the stage on fire in *Musical Moments from Chopin* (1947), a comical send-up of famous concert pianist Frederic Chopin's music, costarring Andy Panda and Woody Woodpecker; the inebriated mouse "weaving to and fro" in the *Andy Panda* short, *Mousie Come Home* (1946), in which Andy and his dog Milo try trapping the annoying little mouse; and the climactic gag of Woody suffering a "nervous breakdown" in *Knock Knock* (1940). As Walter later stated, "When we got through cutting this one, what was left didn't make much sense."

Meanwhile, Kellogg's entirely rejected the *Swing Symphony* cartoon, *Abu Ben Boogie* (1944), on the grounds that a seductively suggestive dancing harem girl was offensive. They also suggested that Walter retitle the nursery rhyme cartoon, *Three Blind Mice*, a more politically correct, *Three Lazy Mice*. Discussing some of the problems in making his cartoons "pass muster" for television after undergoing such strict censorship, Walter noted in a 1957 *Hollywood Reporter* article: "The first thing that happened was the elimination in one swoop of all my films that contained Negro characters; there were eight such pictures. But we never offended or degraded the colored race and they were all top musical cartoons, too."

As Walter continued, "The [advertising] agency reason was that if there was a question at all on a scene, why leave it in? It might cause some group or other to bring pressure . . ."

Working under the restrictions of this thriving new medium, Walter became particularly choosey about which films he selected featuring Woody. While they were all previously approved by movie censors before their theatrical release, he and his staff also screened them carefully "now that Woody goes right into the living room. There's often a moral lesson involved. And even though Woody is bad sometimes . . . he always gets punished."

BECOMING A TELEVISION HIT

On October 3, 1957, *The Woody Woodpecker Show* made its debut. Walter once described it as, "A real homey show with no tricks." It bowed Thursday afternoons at 5 P.M. PST on ABC, right before Walt Disney's *The Mickey Mouse Club*, which had been shortened from an hour to a half-hour, with Woody assuming the other half-hour in an hour-long time slot. Each half-hour episode featured three theatrical cartoons with segments of Woody, who served as the official host-announcer, along with late-1940s films starring Andy Panda and Oswald the Lucky Rabbit. Walter appeared in live-action segments (seven in all in the first 26 shows) directed by former Disney director Jack Hannah, experienced in directing live-action and animation sequences from his time at Disney studios. The opening of each show combined cartoon and live footage of Woody and Walter together, with his beloved red-topped, blue-feathered woodpecker introducing him to viewers as "My boss, Walter Lantz."

In the premiere episode, Walter reenacted the tale of how Woody came into being, inspired by the story of the real rooftop invader that

Opening cel animation for Lantz's *The Woody Woodpecker Show* he originally produced for ABC in 1957. © *Walter Lantz Productions. All rights reserved.*

disturbed Walter and Grace on their honeymoon. Bracketed between new live-action and animation segments were three theatrical cartoons shown that first week, Woody Woodpecker's *Who's Cooking Who* (1944); the *Musical Miniatures* cartoon, *The Overture to William Tell* (1947), with Wally Walrus masquerading as a famed orchestra leader; and the Andy Panda short, *Life Begins for Andy Panda* (1939), tracing the birth of the cute Chinese cub, which had marked his screen debut.

In live-action wraparounds before and after the cartoons, Walter demonstrated for viewers how Woody and his friends, and animated cartoons in general, were drawn and filmed. He also showed how characters moved, how stories were created, how expressions fit the characters, and what motivated him to create Woody's wild cartoon adventures. Plus, he covered the production pipeline involved in making them—the cutters, the animators, the storyboards, and more—with Woody kibitzing with his famous creator as he gave young viewers simple drawing lessons. In discussing the series, Walter's fondest memories were of the live segments he filmed telling the story of cartoon animation. As he once said, "It was *a first* for television. We showed the entire process of cartoon animation. The first segment was how I discovered Woody Woodpecker, and I made the first drawings of how Woody looked at the different stages. Every segment after that was five minutes showing every phase of cartoon production. The first was how Woody was created. Then, the next one showed how Andy Panda was created, and then we showed every phase: how a director worked on a storyboard, how the animation was done, inking and painting, sound, recording, and the voice artists. To my knowledge, it has never been done since!"

The series was not only timely and entertaining for children and adult viewers but also became yet another huge, profitable venture for Walter and his studio. "In the early days, we got a lot of fan mail. It slowly petered out, but built up again when we went on television," Walter later said.

Garnering a 25 Nielsen rating each week, *The Woody Woodpecker Show* made Woody a television favorite. The tremendous public response resulted in a flurry of offers from companies to produce Woody Woodpecker merchandise. Suddenly Woody became a super spokes-bird for commercials pitching bread, cereals, and free kazoos. He received around 500 letters a week, excluding Valentine's and Christmas cards, from youngsters all over the country addressed to him in care of the Lantz studio, asking "where Woody sleeps, where he eats, and whether he's just as fresh at home as he is in the movies." In light of Woody's extraordinary popularity with audiences, Walter said then, "It's hard to think of Woody in terms of paper and pencil. He's quite real. . . a likeable, mischievous little character."

Despite his show's success, with dwindling profits from theatrical cartoons still an issue, Walter did not foresee any new and emerging cartoon producers or start-up studios entering the field any time soon. "To start out today, it would cost a firm $40,000 for each six-minute short," he told staff writer Hal Morris of *The Daily Mirror* of Los Angeles in 1957, "and there are many obstacles in the way. It takes four years of showings to break even . . . And if it weren't for reissues [about every seven years of his old cartoons], I'd be out of business."

With *The Woody Woodpecker Show* generating new revenue, Walter was so busy he could not even think of retiring and continued to produce new *Woody Woodpecker* cartoons, introducing that August a new breakout costar with Woody, Gabby Gator, and others for the theaters along with his hit television series. "If TV hadn't come along," he later said, "there would be a very sad picture in the cartoon industry."

On September 25, 1958, ABC cancelled *The Woody Woodpecker Show* after only one season. By February 1959, with the countrymen of more than 70 nations, even Russia, knowing his raucous laugh intimately, the series—retitled *Woody Woodpecker and Friends* (and later as *Woody Woodpcker and His Friends*)—began airing in syndication on independent stations across the country until 1966. On Los Angeles's KTTV Channel 11, the program was broadcast Sundays during dinner hour at six o'clock, starting with the first episode featuring the 1947 cartoon, *Woody the Giant Killer*. Of the success of his sassy woodpecker and his world-famous laugh, Walter said at the time, "He laughed me to fame, too, not to mention the crew of 52 artists and technicians who keep Woody laughing."

Woody Woodpecker and Friends remained a top daytime television series, attracting a new audience every two years. At that rate, Walter predicted, "Woody will run forever."

Certainly, at the time, it appeared Walter would be right. The series and its onslaught of licensed merchandise, including games, novelties, clothing, and some 3 million comic books sold each year bearing the likenesses of Woody, paid him a steady stream of revenues in royalties from each sale and residuals earned from his cartoons. Walter's stature around the world rose dramatically as a result. During a

Among the many licensing opportunities spurred by the success of Lantz's television series, Woody Woodpecker was featured in a two-page advertisement for Roman Meal Bread in 1959.

promotional trip to Tokyo in 1961 with Grace, much to his delight they were engulfed by 28 reporters, and radio and television people, wanting to interview them and asking for Grace to do her famous Woody laugh.

STILL MAKING HIS MARK

With hardly anyone making theatrical cartoons anymore, Walter remained the most active producer. In September 1959, he added three new characters to his roster—two troublemaking mice cast opposite a highly sophisticated cat—in a series of misadventures, *Hickory, Dickory, and Doc.* A year later, he released to theaters *Fatso the*

Bear, reviving director Jack Hannah's "dumb" Humphrey the Bear, which he had created and helmed in the 1950s for Disney. The series ran its course after only three cartoons released through 1961. With 19 cartoons scheduled for release in 1961, including eight *Woody Woodpeckers* and three *Chilly Willys,* Walter treated audiences to three installments of a second brand-new series: the droopy-eyed, bushy-mustached, and laconic-voiced secret agent, *Inspector Willoughby* (originally appearing as an unnamed security guard in 1958's *Salmon Yeggs*). In 1962, he produced his third new series in as many years made expressly for movie theaters, *The Beary Family* (originally titled *It's the Bearys*), inspired by the popular live-action sitcom *The Life of Riley.* The series followed the everyday lives and misadventures of a bear family—dad Charlie, mother Bessie, son Junior, and daughter Suzy. It lasted 10 years besides being repackaged for television as a separate 13-episode series until Walter closed his studio's doors in 1972. It became one of only three regular theatrical cartoon series he produced after 1966.

Given the weak financial footing for theatrical cartoons and financial mortality rate of their makers, this feat was nothing short of astonishing. The animation industry had become a graveyard for many a bright hope and for many practitioners who had once dreamed of fame and fortune only to fail. One reason in large part for his continuing success was that Walter employed the same down-to-earth business practices he learned early his career: staying within a budget, promoting the product, developing loyal workers, and keeping his eye on the details.

As one of Hollywood's happiest teams—in marriage, at work, and at play—Walter and Grace continued living their lives to the fullest. As Grace once said in an interview, "We're always having fun."

Part of that came from always keeping things in proper balance in their lives. With work requiring four or five hours a day of his time, Walter lived up to his belief, "You've got to have hobbies." Two of his favorites were fishing and golfing. Grace shared his love of fishing on a boat they owned. One of Walter's most famous catches was hooking a 110-pound sailfish with a light line. But Grace did not warm up to the idea of spending time on the links with her husband, calling it "a man's game." For relaxation, Walter had taken up another hobby—oil painting—doing mostly still lifes.

As for any thought of retirement, Walter remarked around that time, "As long as I can entertain children, I'll keep going."

During a weekend getaway in 1962, to the gambling capital of the world, Las Vegas, Walter and Grace were out on the links when they heard the devastating news: A raging brushfire had swept through the upscale Bel Air district and destroyed 480 homes, including theirs, which was burned to ashes. Their home and George Pal's were the first destroyed in the inferno, while the home of their next-door neighbor, fellow animator Joe Barbera, was spared. Where most people would have immediately fled to the scene of the disaster, Walter and Grace ordered a bottle of Champagne and enjoyed a sumptuous Italian dinner and then drove home. As Walter later joked with a reporter in reliving the incident, "We enjoy everything—even catastrophes."

Actually, once the Lantzes returned from the trip, they found things were much worse than feared. "We were wiped out . . . and when we got home we didn't have so much as a teaspoon left," Walter later said.

Many of Walter's original paintings were, unfortunately, among the items destroyed. After rebuilding and living in the same area of Bel Air until 1967, the couple moved into a brand-new hilltop home in the Trousdale Estates that Walter designed. A reflection of his comfort and beauty, the rambling estate featured many displays of Walter's original oil paintings in the dining and living rooms, bedrooms and hallway, which they affectionately dubbed their "galleria," and the private studio in which he painted. The place had all the accoutrements they wanted and was well appointed throughout, including closets built for their height and reach ("Walter had everything made so I can reach—I'm only 5 feet and I have trouble with the usual shelves," Grace enthused) and an extravagant bathtub in their master bathroom that was not sunken, unlike the usual status symbol in most upscale homes back then. "I didn't want a sunken tub," Grace giggled in telling a reporter. "I guess I'm not really from Trousdale."

Promotional still of Woody Woodpecker and company for a later incarnation of Lantz's widely syndicated television series, renamed *Woody Woodpecker and His Friends. (Courtesy: Walter Lantz)* © Walter Lantz Productions. All rights reserved.

For the last decade or more that he produced original theatrical cartoons, Walter stopped entering his films for Oscar consideration in the "Best Short-Subject" category. As he put it, "I was disappointed with the type of cartoons the Academy was giving awards to. You couldn't class the type of cartoons we and Warners, MGM, and Disney were making just for laughs with pieces animated by [John] Hubley and others. And we couldn't get nominations anymore. These other cartoons were beating us out, so I didn't turn in any [films] for over 10 years."

By 1964, its fifth season in syndication, Walter repackaged *Woody Woodpecker and Friends*, adding new color films from the late 1950s and the 1960s along with the adventures of Andy Panda, Chilly Willy, Maw and Paw, The Foolish Fables, and Sugarfoot. Two cartoons, each originally made as unaired television series pilots and instead previously released theatrically in 1960, also made their TV debut, *Jungle Medics*, starring a pair of chimps, Sam 'n' Simian, and *The Secret Weapon*, marking the first appearance of Space Mouse, a character created by Craig Chase for Walter Lantz's comic books. Walter also filmed some new introductions for this syndicated edition as well two new segments, one of which featured newsreels of major events in history. The other, called "Around the World with Woody," featured around-the-globe films illustrating life in other countries as narrated by Walter and his bird pal Woody.

That same season Walter hosted and produced a special Halloween episode of *Woody Woodpecker and Friends*, "Spook-a-Nanny," in which he and his world-famous animated friends throw a Halloween party. Sandwiched between showings of such classic cartoons as *Under the Counter Spy* (1954) and *Playful Pelican* (1948) were new live-action and animated segments of Walter and Woody preparing for the party and concluding with the all-new six-minute cartoon "Spook-a-Nanny," starring Woody and many other Lantz characters singing and dancing to the tune of the same name.

On Wednesday, May 24, 1967, Walter, the last of the pioneer cartoonists still active in the industry, was feted with a luncheon at Universal Studios in honor of his 50th anniversary in the motion picture medium. In attendance were numerous film industry luminaries and dignitaries, including Universal vice president in charge of production Edward Muhl, producer George Pal, fellow animation legends Joe Barbera and Dave Fleischer, and Universal City mayor Karen Jensen. Charles Boren, executive vice president of Motion Picture and Television Producers, presented the gray-fringed, 68-year-old animator, flanked by his lovely wife Grace, with a gold statuette of Woody Woodpecker for "continuous and dedicated contributions to the cartoon industry for the past 50 years." The event also marked the 25th birthday of Walter's cackling cartoon bird, still flickering across movie and television screens and then popular in 72 countries and syndicated on television in 200 American and 40 foreign markets abroad.

Following the awards presentation and speeches, a birthday cake was rolled out with one symbolic candle for Walter to blow out. Afterward, they posed for pictures with two young Woody Woodpecker fans seated at a special table. During a break in the festivities, Walter spoke to the press and gave no indication of retiring. Instead, he said with a smile, "I'm just starting. In another 11 years I'll be here [at Universal] for 50 years. I hope I last 50 more."

Of her 17-year association as the voice of Woody, Grace later joked with a reporter, "Yeah, I'm strictly for the birds."

With still many of his top studio people under his employ for 25 years, Walter had the luxury of knowing he did not have to work so hard anymore and stayed home and painted in the mornings in his elegant studio at home—or as Grace called it, the "house that Woody Woodpecker built." Of his studio situated with views of Beverly Hills and the

Lantz creates and signs an original drawing of Woody Woodpecker for a young fan, Greg Lenburg, during a visit to Universal Studios in the summer of 1967. *(Photo by John L. Lenburg)* © *Greg Lenburg Collection*

Pacific Ocean, Walter said, "This is my garret—you think a poor artist can paint here?"

One painting he had in the works was a still-life oil portrait of Grace, who did not hold back her opinion; she told her famous husband how to paint it to the point she would become breathless. She was partly dissatisfied with the results, saying that "nobody knows it's me because my mouth is shut."

Much to his amazement, Walter's still-life paintings sold for $500 apiece at a gallery in 1967. That year he produced 13 new theatrical cartoon shorts and 26 half-hour shows for television and dubbed dialogue with Grace for *Woody Woodpecker* cartoons. In August, he and Grace traveled to appear at Montreal's Expo '67, which was saluting Walter for his pioneering work as a cartoon producer. Enjoying living in their new home, both were conflicted about making the trip. As Grace said, "We really hate to leave. We love this house so."

Although the couple never had any children of their own, Grace added, "Thanks to Woody Woodpecker, we've got millions."

In November 1968, after painting landscapes and marine and still lifes for more than a quarter century, 69-year-old Walter put many of his oil paintings on display at the McKenzie Art Gallery at 861 N. La Cienega Boulevard in Los Angeles through the Christmas season. Happy to share his work with the world, he noted at the time that the "greatest sin" an amateur artist can make is "blindly falling in love with his own painting and giving it to another human being who might not appreciate it.

"Art is such a personal thing," he said. "What one person enjoys, another will dislike. The value of any given piece of art cannot honestly be predicted when individual tastes are concerned because there is no true barometer that gives accurate readings of the heart." He added, "And the heart, after all, is of major importance in determining the intrinsic value of any work of art."

Walter, who became interested in art in 1911, offered his suggestions to amateur artists on what questions they could ask themselves before giving away their "labor of love" to others. As he told *The Los Angeles*

One of Lantz's favorite pastimes, seen here in 1968, was painting in his home studio still-life paintings that sold for top dollar at art galleries. © *AP*

Times: "Will my painting be sincerely appreciated? Is my work worthy of hanging on his living room wall, or will it wind up as a dust catcher in the garbage? Is my gift an imposition, or an enlightening experience?"

Always one who gave back to his community, Walter's life took on greater importance in the months ahead as he and Grace would spread joy and laughter in other parts of the world to those who needed it the most.

The Last Reel

In November of 1969, with emotions running high over the continued deaths of American servicemen during the Vietnam War, Walter and his wife Grace embarked on one of the most rewarding adventures of their lives ("It was the most gratifying thing we've done," Walter later related). After Grace, who had volunteered for 15 years as a Red Cross Grey Lady, read in a magazine article about the tremendous need for entertainers to entertain wounded service men, she and Walter set out on a USO-sponsored "handshake tour." They brightened the lives of 5,600 wounded G.I.s at 24 military hospitals under the U.S. Pacific Naval command in Japan, the Philippines, Guam, Okinawa, Korea, and other Pacific Rim countries.

Flying 30,000 miles and touring for a weary 31 straight days, they stopped and chatted at the bedside of hospitalized servicemen at every stop. After entering the hospital wards, Walter would introduce himself, saying, "Hi fellas. I'm Walter Lantz. This is Gracie, my wife, the voice of Woody Woodpecker. We're here from Hollywood just to shake your hands and let you know we're thinking about you."

The response to their presence was far greater than both had imagined. The famed 70-year-old motion picture animator ended up drawing literally thousands of Woody Woodpecker caricatures—on post

Lantz signs a three-year extension in the company of Universal Studios vice president Ed Muhl. Lantz enjoyed the longest producer–studio association of any producer with a single studio in industry history.

cards, photos, and plaster casts—to the delight of seriously injured and bedridden servicemen. Many joked and laughed and asked the star couple how cartoons were made, as his spry 66-year-old wife performed her machine-gun Woody laugh upon request "thousands of times" with some patients recording her famous bird laugh. One actually threatened to "blast" his recording at 4 A.M. to "shake up the doctors."

After returning to the United States, the happy couple urged other well-known show business figures to volunteer their time and energy in similar fashion as they entertained many more veterans and servicemen hospitalized at VA facilities across the country.

As the oldest producer of movie cartoons after more than four decades with the same studio, the craggy-faced, raspy-voiced 71-year-old animator kept pecking away at the business that bestowed him so much joy, up to his usual tricks, still going "for laughs." On September 12, 1970, 13 years after its original network run, *The Woody Woodpecker Show*, still popular on television screens overseas, returned to network television when NBC added it to its Saturday morning schedule. The show lasted seven seasons until September 3, 1977. With Woody's physical appearance slightly altered and updated, Walter assembled an additional 26 half-hour episodes, minus his live-action hosting segments, from his studio's post-1948 cartoons. The series featured his famous beaked troublemaker, Woody, and the cartoon comedies *Inspector Willoughby*, *Foolish Fables*, *Maw and Paw*, *Space Mouse*, *Sugarfoot*, and *Chilly Willy*. He also included in this second network installment the live-action segment *Woody's Newsreel*, formerly titled *Around the World with Woody* in the syndicated version, in which Walter showed comical scenes from vintage movie newsreel films, once again introduced by Woody.

The continuing appeal of his tassel-topped, cackling character, in Walter's opinion, was that the material really did not date itself because "we use no puns or popular phrases of the time; also, they are made up of two-thirds physical and sight gags and only one-third dialogue." He said further that this was the "secret" behind Woody's success in foreign countries, where "we don't even translate the dialogue."

Walter emphasized that audiences embraced Woody and many of his cartoon creations because his films never went for "violence per se. Physical gags, yes; a character may be all banged up in one scene but he's all right in the next scene. And we never show blood." Unlike earlier interviews in his career in describing Woody, his perception of his famous character had evolved and mellowed with age. As he told Philip K. Scheuer of *The Los Angeles Times* in 1969: "How would I explain

Woody? Well, he was very raucous to start with, but he evolved as he went along. It's very difficult to say of a cartoon character, this is it—and since he's not human we can take a lot of liberties. I think 'precocious' is the word for him now; he goes along minding his own business until someone tries to take advantage of him; he likes to do the things we all would, only we don't have the courage."

Although the fundamentals of his hammering woodpecker had changed, the fundamentals of producing 13 new theatrical cartoon shorts a year remained the same. Each six-minute short took him and his small staff of 30 animators and artists four months to complete

Lantz's Woody Woodpecker continued to produce laughs on movie screens in new color cartoon shorts until production ceased in 1972, the year Lantz closed his Hollywood cartoon studio. © *Walter Lantz Productions. All rights reserved.*

from script to screen. Situations were neither old-fashioned nor controversial but instead as topical as "taking a camping trip or installing a TV set," requiring about 5,000 drawings per cartoon to animate as opposed 1,200 for a television cartoon of the same length. Unlike the minimally animated television cartoons that spared moving parts for its characters, Walter proudly stated, "Our characters act out the whole line with hands and bodies, not in the jerky movements of part-time animation."

Walter was proud of the fact his studio had outlasted many other major cartoon studios with whom he once competed. As he once said, "Walt Disney got up to $100,000 for a six-minute short and quit doing them. MGM [home of Tom and Jerry and others] was spending $55,000 to $60,000 and closed down. I am the only one left with my business—financing, producing..." He attributed his continuing success to the fact that he had a backlog of films still creating revenue and working for him and "only if you have one—you can come out [ahead] on your investment."

While several independent animators had entered the fray producing feature-length cartoons to compete with Disney, after making about 1,100 cartoons in his career—195 of them *Woody Woodpeckers*—Walter had no desire to follow suit. "Very few, outside of Disney's, have ever been successful," he stated, "and his have come to $3 or $4 million apiece. Even with a one-shot deal, if you miss, you can lose everything you've worked for the last 40 years."

CELEBRATING A CARTOON LEGEND

Going full-steam despite their advancing years, in 1971, Walter and Grace celebrated Woody's 30th birthday of his first "official" self-titled cartoon, *Woody Woodpecker*, in style. Among the number of activities to mark the occasion, Woody was honored as part of a six-week exhibit on the art of animation at the California Museum of Science and Industry in Los Angeles, as were Walter, Grace, and Woody in on-the-air tributes by many leading film and television personalities.

More honors and tributes followed. In June 1972, Walter and Grace were honored as guests at the Animated Film Festival in Zagreb,

Yugoslavia, the same month the Yugoslavian government issued a new Woody Woodpecker commemorative stamp. The tribute included screenings of many of Walter's cartoons and a special exhibit Walter created demonstrating the complex process of making animated film. Reflecting on his accomplishments during his career after returning to United States, Walter stated around this time, "To me the most satisfying thing about all these years in the cartoon business is all the entertainment I've brought to people. No messages. Just pure entertainment."

On November 29, 1973, after more than a half-century of entertaining generations of cartoons lovers throughout the world, Walter was hailed once again. This time the Hollywood chapter of the Association Internationale du Film D'Animation (ASIFA), the largest animation industry organization in the world in only its second year of existence, presented the pioneer animator with its Winsor McCay lifetime achievement award. One of ASIFA's highest honors, the McCay award is given to individuals in the animation industry in recognition of their tremendous career contributions to the art of animation, at the Sportsmen's Lodge located in the heart of Studio City, a suburb of Los Angeles.

Because of his relatively high production, Walter succeeded where other cartoons producers had not and became the longest-running producer of theatrical cartoons up until 1972, when his studio ceased production and he laid off his staff. In the current business climate, Walter found it was no longer feasible to produce cartoons for the theaters and expect to recoup production costs quickly. As he once said, "It sometimes took up to three years to realize your costs back. That was after publicity and distribution costs. There just wasn't any money left in theatrical cartoons. To produce them right today would cost about $90,000 a cartoon. When I saw that I couldn't do it anymore, that's when I decided to take a hiatus."

Although no longer animating new cartoons, Walter remained in business. He prepared new cartoon packages for television, supervised licensing of his famous cartoon characters, and lectured at colleges and animation festivals. Meanwhile Universal continued to reissue about

Lantz poses with comedian Robin Williams after being awarded an honorary Oscar at the 51st annual Academy Awards in April 1979, 18 days shy of his 80th birthday. © *The Academy of Motion Picture Arts & Sciences. All rights reserved.*

13 old cartoons a year, some generating as much revenue as they did when they were originally released. By 1977, Walter's 55th year as a producer, a record unmatched by other active producers of animation and live-action films, NBC marked his anniversary in appropriate fashion with the return of *The Woody Woodpecker Show* on Saturday mornings, starting on September 11 at 8:00 A.M. This final season rebroadcast the films from the 1970–1971 season, sans *Woody's Newsreel* and later additions, including *The Beary Family* (1962–1971) and *Hickory, Dickory, and Doc* (1959–1962). That same year, additional unaired cartoons were bundled with the original series for syndication as *Woody Woodpecker and Friends*.

Still leading busy and active lives, that year Walter and Grace attended the Special Olympics in Los Angeles, finding "something more rewarding than producing cartoons." Grace performed her famous Woody laugh, and the couple posed for pictures with some of the 2,600 handicapped children competing in numerous sporting events. Walter was also honored that year by New York's Museum of Modern Art with a retrospective of his career. A year later, Filmdex in Los Angeles repeated the honor. As he later said, "It's been a wonderful life in this business, bringing laughs to so many people. I've never had anything to sell but humor."

Recognizing his astonishing career, at the 51st annual Academy Awards held on April 9, 1979, at the Dorothy Chandler Pavilion, the Motion Picture Academy of Arts and Science awarded Walter, 18 days shy of his 80th birthday, a long overdue honor: an Honorary Academy Award for his technical achievements in the field of cartoon animation. The award was rather fitting, especially since all he wanted to do throughout his career was to entertain people. As Walter recalled, "I was really very much surprised. In fact, I was so pleased that I did some animation of Woody—at my own expense—accepting the Oscar with me. It was just a great, great honor."

A year later in an exclusive interview, Walter was proud of the fact his studio was "still very much in business," with reissues of his theatrical cartoons still playing in around 12,000 theaters in the United

Lantz pauses for a photograph in front of a disco poster of Woody Woodpecker in his office, circa 1980. © *Jeff Lenburg. All rights reserved.*

States and in about 80 different countries, including his syndicated *Woody Woodpecker and Friends* playing all over Europe. "Although we are not producing new material," he said in an interview, "we are releasing our old cartoons and still have several hundred cartoons that have never been shown on television. So every two years, I make up a new package."

Walter did not close the door on possibly going into production again. As he added, "As a comparable cartoon for television, it's quite possible."

In the meantime, Walter continued working on his second career. Besides minding his studio, he devoted much of his spare time to painting. His works, largely still lifes of his characters in landscapes with Woody, sold for tens and thousands of dollars in animation art galleries in Hawaii and New York, and in auctions at charity benefits throughout the country. Also issued were pewter statues of his legendary cartoon characters and collector plates of Woody spoofing famous paintings, along with toys, dolls, and comic books. As Walter explained, "I'm using Woody Woodpecker in my paintings. I use authentic backgrounds and put my characters in them doing different things in these paintings. So I'm at another career at 80 years old. Isn't that fabulous!"

In the spring of 1982, the warm, genial 82-year-old animator renewed his distribution contract with Universal through 1987, after first signing with them in 1929, making it Hollywood's longest-running contract. The deal called for Universal to reissue 13 old theatrical cartoons each year and for the release of another 190 cartoons never-before-seen on television via syndication. Later that spring they opened a special exhibit honoring Walter at Universal Studios theme park featuring film clips, a display on how animation is made, and a collection of memorabilia from his storied career. That Thanksgiving, a 75-foot balloon replica of Woody also debuted as it floated down Fifth Avenue in the annual Macy's Thanksgiving Day Parade along with a larger-than-life balloon of Popeye's famous girlfriend, Olive Oyl, becoming the first female character in the parade's history.

That same month, the sounds of Walter's famous laughing woodpecker were enshrined in the Smithsonian Institute in Washington,

Lantz signs a copy of his authorized biography, *The Walter Lantz Story*, with Grace at his side in November 1988. *(Courtesy: Raymond Cox).*

D.C., as Walter turned over 17 artifacts to its Natural Museum of American History, including a wooden model of Woody and a storyboard for the initial 1940 cartoon, *Knock Knock*. Fittingly, Grace made her entrance, creating the character's unforgettable laugh during ceremonies to mark the occasion.

On March 5, 1986, after bringing hours of laughter and entertainment to generations of fans, the 86-year-old legendary animator finally received his very own bronze star on the Hollywood Walk of Fame, located at 7000 Hollywood Boulevard right next to film legend Errol

Lantz, later in life, with a pint-sized Woody Woodpecker on his shoulder. *(Courtesy: Royal Art Galleries)*

Flynn. Accompanied by Grace and a costumed Woody Woodpecker, he beamed proudly during its unveiling and afterward as Hollywood's honorary Mayor Johnny Grant presented him with a small-sized replica.

After 60 years of marriage, Walter's wife and actress, Grace Lantz, who provided Woody's voice and boisterous laugh from 1950 to 1972, and periodically until 1985, sadly breathed her last. She died on March 17, 1992, at age 88.

Without his wife at his side, Walter kept active until his death five years later, on March 22, 1994, one month shy of his 95th birthday, of heart failure at St. Joseph's Medical Center in nearby Burbank, a suburb of Los Angeles. He and Grace were both interred at Forest Lawn Memorial Park in Hollywood Hills.

Looking back on his life and career, Walter had no regrets—just fond memories of an industry that would never be the same. As he said, "I've had so many wonderful moments in this business and the business has been very good to me. It's very hard to pick out one thing that's been great. But, you know, I've had my hits and misses on pictures. But I will say one thing, I've had more of my share of hits than misses."

SELECTED RESOURCES

For further study of Walter Lantz's career and work, the following resources are recommended:

Filmographies

The Walter Lantz Cartune Encyclopedia (http://lantz. goldenagecartoons.com/)

This Web site features complete and detailed listings, including credits and release dates, of every Walter Lantz sound cartoon made from 1929 to 1972.

Walter Lantz Filmography (http://www.imdb.com/name/ nm0487237/)

Produced by imdb.com, this Web page features a complete filmography of Walter Lantz's career, categorized by year and by category—producer, director, actor, and writer—from silent to sound cartoons and television.

DVD and Home Video Collections

Woody Woodpecker Favorites (Columbia House, 2009)

This single-disc "best of" compilation is comprised entirely of 20 shorts included as part of 2007's *The Woody Woodpecker and Friends Classic Cartoon Collection, Volume 1*, from the 1940 *Andy Panda* cartoon, *Knock Knock*, marking the debut of Woody Woodpecker, to the 1945

Swing Symphony cartoon, *Pied Piper of Basin Street*. Other bonus features include episodes #53 and #56 of *The Woody Woodpecker Show*.

Woody Woodpecker and Friends Classic Cartoon Collection, Vol. 1 (Universal Studios Home Entertainment, 2007)

This first of two three-disc DVD collections offers 75 Walter Lantz theatrical cartoons produced from 1940 to 1956, including the first 45 *Woody Woodpecker* cartoons and 30 other cartoons featuring Andy Panda, Chilly Willy, and Oswald the Lucky Rabbit, and from Lantz's *Swing Symphonies* and *Cartune Classics* series. Additional bonus material includes *Walter, Woody, and the World of Animation: The Walter Lantz Story; Cartoonland Mysteries*, a 1936 documentary newsreel on Lantz's studio from Universal's *Going Places* series; six "Behind-the-Scenes" segments with Lantz from *The Woody Woodpecker Show* (1957); and the rarely seen special Halloween TV episode, "Spook-a-Nanny."

Woody Woodpecker and Friends Classic Cartoon Collection, Vol. 2 (Universal Studios Home Entertainment, 2008)

This three-disc set, continuing from Vol. 1 in the series, features 75 cartoon shorts produced by Walter Lantz Productions from 1932 to 1958, including the next 45 *Woody Woodpecker* cartoons, plus five *Andy Panda* shorts, five *Chilly Willy* shorts, five *Oswald the Lucky Rabbit* shorts, five *Musical Favorites*, and 10 *Cartune Classics*. Bonus features include 12 "Behind-the-Scenes" segments with Walter Lantz from 1957's *The Woody Woodpecker Show*; the cartoons originally made as pilots for possible series: *The Secret Weapon* featuring for the first time Space Mouse, and *Jungle Medics* starring the chimps Sam 'n' Simian; and episode #47 of *The Woody Woodpecker Show*.

SELECTED BIBLIOGRAPHY

Adamson, Joe. *The Walter Lantz Story with Woody Woodpecker and Friends*. New York: G.P. Putnam's Sons, 1985.

Ames, Walter. "Cartoon Factory on KTTV; Loud Outfit Worn by Cronyn." *Los Angeles Times*. April 5, 1957.

"Animation Group to Fete Lantz." *Los Angeles Times*. September 25, 1973.

"Cartunes for Europe." *Motion Picture Herald*. June 2, 1943, 33.

Churchill, Douglas W. "Hollywood Reports: Columbia Considers Filming the 'Lost Atlantis'—Noting the Draft Cycle." *New York Times*. November 17, 1940.

Culhane, Shamus. *Talking Animals and Other People*. Cambridge, Mass.: Da Capo Press, 1998.

Giller, Philip, and John Alyn. "Memories of a Wonderful Man." *In Toon*. Spring 1994, Vol. 1.

Greenfield, Allan. "Frame by Frame." *Classic Images*. January 1980.

"Happy Hollywood Team Owns Woody Woodpecker." *The Hartford Courant*. May 21, 1967.

Hopper, Hedda. "Hollywood." *The Hartford Courant*. December 2, 1954.

———. "Woody Woodpecker Runs Afoul of Censors." *Los Angeles Times*. November 30, 1954.

"Humanettes Offered by Lantz as Novelty." *Motion Picture Herald*. June 2, 1943, 33.

"Lantz Honored by Universal Studios." *Los Angeles Times*. May 26, 1967.

Lantz, Walter. "'Merry Christmas' It's a Wish from Woody Woodpecker." *Los Angeles Times*. December 3, 1967.

Le Baron, Boots. "Artist Lantz' Advice to Amateurs." *Los Angeles Times*. November 28, 1968.

Leap, Norris. "Outlook People: Failure to Raise $14,000 Helped Cartoonist Lantz Double Fortune." *Los Angeles Times*. March 26, 1961.

Lenburg, Jeff. *The Encyclopedia of Animated Cartoons*, 3d ed. New York: Facts On File, 2009.

———. *The Great Cartoon Directors*. Cambridge, Mass.: Da Capo Press, 1993.

"Lilting Laughter? Raucous, Sassy Woody Woodpecker Is a She." *Los Angeles Times*. May 10, 1959.

Maltin, Leonard. *Of Mice and Magic: A History of American Animated Cartoons*. New York: Plume, 1987.

McFadden, Irwin S. "HaHaHaHaHa!" *Flashback*. September 1972.

McMurphy, Jean. "TV Success Gives Ha Ha Ha Woody Reason to Laugh." *Los Angeles Times*. April 20, 1958.

Morris, Hal. "Cartoon Future Dim, Says Walter Lantz." *Daily Mirror*. October 18, 1957.

Naughton, Russ. "Record Ramblings." *The Hartford Courant*. June 13, 1948.

———. "Record Ramblings." *The Hartford Courant*. June 27, 1948.

———. "Record Ramblings." *The Hartford Courant*. May 23, 1948.

Parrott, Jennings. "Newsmakers: He Always Sounded as If He Belonged in an Institution." *Los Angeles Times*. November 17, 1982.

Peary, Danny, and Gerald Peary. *The American Animated Cartoon: A Critical Anthology*. New York: E.P. Dutton, 1980.

Scheurer, Philip K. "Walter Lantz Draws His Cartoons Just for Laughs." *Los Angeles Times*. November 23, 1969.

———. "Studios Theater Gossip." *Los Angeles Times*. May 21, 1939.

Schallert, Edwin. "Screen: 'Andy Panda' Producer Plans Feature Cartoon." *Los Angeles Times*. December 23, 1939.

Smith, Cecil. "TV's Woody Woodpecker Begins Tonight." *Los Angeles Times*. February 22, 1959.

Solomon, Charles. "Lantz: A Career as Laugh Maker." *Los Angeles Times*. April 13, 1982.

Vils, Ursula. "Lantzes Flying High with Woody Woodpecker." *Los Angeles Times*. August 21, 1967.

Walter Lantz, interview by author, September 10, 1980.

"Walter Lantz." *Films in Review*. April 1971.

"Woody Woodpecker Scores Hit with GI's." *The Hartford Courant*. January 18, 1970.

"Woody Woodpecker Show Is Lesson in Cartooning." *The Hartford Courant*. November 10, 1957.

"Yugoslavian Government Planning Special Woody Woodpecker Stamp." *The Hartford Courant*. January 9, 1972.

INDEX

129

ABOUT THE AUTHOR

Jeff Lenburg is an award-winning author, celebrity biographer, and nationally acknowledged expert on animated cartoons who has spent nearly three decades researching and writing about this lively art. He has written nearly 30 books—including such acclaimed histories of animation as *Who's Who in Animated Cartoons*, *The Great Cartoon Directors*, and four previous encyclopedias of animated cartoons. His books have been nominated for several awards, including the American Library Association's "Best Non-Fiction Award" and the Evangelical Christian Publishers Association's Gold Medallion Award for "Best Autobiography/Biography." He lives in Arizona.

Photo courtesy: Brian Maurer.